MODERN PRAIRIE

sewing

20 Handmade Projects for You & Your Friends

Abigail A. Long

stash BOOKS.

an imprint of C&T Publishing

Publisher: Amy Marson

Creative Director: Gailen Runge

Art Director: Kristy Zacharias

Book Designer: April Mostek

Page Layout Artist: Katie McIntosh

Editors: S. Michele Fry and Monica Gyulai

Technical Editors: Alison M. Schmidt and Gailen Runge

Production Coordinator: Jenny Davis

Production Editor: Katie Van Amburg

Illustrator: Valyrie Gillum

Photo Assistant: Mary Peyton Peppo

Styled photography by Nissa Brehmer, unless otherwise noted; Instructional photography by Diane Pedersen, unless otherwise noted

Published by Stash Books, an imprint of C&T Publishing, Inc., P.O. Box 1456, Lafayette, CA 94549

Library of Congress Cataloging-in-Publication Data

Long, Abigail A., 1992-

 Modern prairie sewing : 20 handmade projects for you & your friends / Abigail A. Long.

    pages cm

 ISBN 978-1-60705-878-6 (soft cover)

 1. Sewing. I. Title.

 TT705.L57 2014

 646.4--dc23

                            2013045114

Printed in China

10 9 8 7 6 5 4 3 2 1

Dedication

To Mommy—forever you have sewn, quilted, loved, and made. Your hands will always be beautiful to me. I'll love you forever!

To my grandmothers and their grandmothers before them, who passed on the love of working with their hands. I love you all dearly.

Special Thanks To ...

My parents, for loving me, for being 100 percent behind me, and for thinking everything I make is awesome. You're fabulous and I love you!

My grandparents, for your enthusiasm, words of wisdom, and amazing encouragement! I'm so thankful you're mine and I'm yours. I love you all!

My siblings, Apphia, Achaia, Abiah, Joe, and Charlie. You are hands-down lovable. Apphia and Achaia—thanks for everything, for modeling for me and for always being there. You're the absolute best! Abiah and Joe—for the late, fun nights spent talking and laughing. Joe—thanks for praying for us. Abiah—you're the greatest photographer, pal, confidant, and baby sister in the world. I love you! Charlie, my hilarious man, I love your smile. I love you all lots!

Aunt Amy, for your suggestions and sweet note. The Amy bag would never have come about had it not been for you! Thank you so much. I love you.

My gorgeous models and friends: Faith Cook, Jane Cook, Becky Cook, Apphia Long, Achaia Long, Abiah Long, and Anna Davis. You all are the best models in the world! Thank you so much for your flexibility and for being such amazing friends. This book wouldn't be the same without you!

My amazing testers and friends: Jenny Fish, Sandy Kingery, Anna Davis, Kaitlyn Coghlan, Megan Coghlan, Lydia Coghlan, Natalie Coghlan, Becca Coghlan, Deanna Mullins, and Abiah Long. You really are the best.

The Walton and Cook families, for everything from hilarious game and movie nights to fun hikes and swimming in the creek. Your enthusiasm for and willingness to help with this project have been such a blessing to me. You're awesome friends and I love you all!

Michael Miller fabrics, for supplying me with some really, really adorable fabrics; and QuiltHome, an amazingly gorgeous fabric store with sweet service.

Roxane Cerda, you are priceless! Thank you for everything you did to make this book possible. Michele Fry, you are the best! Thank you for working so hard to keep the book mine. Many thank-yous (and hugs) to the whole C&T Publishing team. You all are so much fun to work with. You're amazing!!

Innumerable thanks, love, hugs, and kisses to all of my family and friends who have added so much to my life and encouraged me as I worked on this project.

Most important, all praise goes to my Lord and Savior, Jesus Christ, for making all of this happen. And for saying, "Yes."

contents

 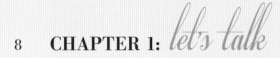
What Anna said about the Amy bag!
"The Amy bag is simple and easy to make. I was able to follow the instructions with ease, and while making it, I learned several new, efficient techniques for making bags. Just for fun I made the Amy bag pocket and put it on the outside of my bag too. It's perfect for everything; from my phone to extra bobby pins. And now, I use my Amy bag often—taking little things along on a trip to town, or carrying my piano books to a lesson. I recommend this book; you will enjoy sewing these unique, exciting patterns!"

What Abiah said about the Betty Pouch!
"The Betty Pouch is so easy and fun to whip up. I *love* the fact that I can use some of my favorite little fabric pieces together. It makes such a cute little gift, too!"

What Jenny said about the Pieces and Letters Pillowcase!

"A fun popcorn party project to work on with a group of friends, or a great gift idea for friends or family. This is a really cute and easy pattern with endless possibilities in fabric combinations."

What Jenny said about the hand towel!

"A quick and easy pattern that makes a great first project for a new sewist or a quick project for a seasoned sewist. Well-thought-out instructions with a fresh take on hand towels."

HELLO, NEW FRIENDS!

Sewing is more than just following a sewing pattern. It elicits excitement and joy. Making something with a simple piece of fabric and thread, making it personal and very much your own—that's exciting! And when it's not for your own home or closet, joy comes from knowing you will bless someone with a gift made with love.

In my family we were (and, I might add, are) always building, painting, sewing, crafting, tearing down (or out) and building again, and sewing even more. In the late 1950s, my great-grandma Daniels made circle skirts for my paternal grandma, Mamaw. In the 70s, my maternal grandma, Nanny, made the majority of my mom's and aunts' clothes. In the 90s, my three sisters and I were always mixing and matching and coordinating the clothes that Mom and Nan made for us. Mommy was always making something, and my two older sisters worked on their own crafts a lot too. My younger sister and I were surrounded and nurtured. When we walked over to my great-grandma Conwell's house, she and my great-aunt pulled out the quilts they were working on and we would run our fingers over the stitches. Another aunt would bring us beautifully crocheted hair knickknacks. We were soon crafting on our own.

As a young girl, I made pillows by the boatload. (Paper towels do work for stuffing!) I was just eight years old when I designed and made my first bag. I recall proudly carrying it to a doctor's appointment. I was too excited to be concerned about the mismatched thread or that it was sewn with the seams out or that I didn't put in a lining. Things have changed a little since then—I do insert linings, and, for the most part, I use matching thread. But one thing hasn't changed: the thrill that comes from inventing something new and useful. I want to share that excitement with you.

I didn't want this book to be complicated, but I didn't want it to be boring and common either. So every project has an unexpected touch—a large flower on the Maggie bag (page 28), big box pleats and large gussets on the KittyJo bag (page 56), and girly but manageable gathers on the clothing. I wanted you to be able to practice the craft of sewing without having to change or add anything to your project to make it special. Regardless of your sewing level, these clever patterns will enable you to make stand-out projects without the need to add or take away anything.

Modern Prairie Sewing is divided into four chapters:

Chapter 1 is where we talk. We talk fabric, threads, sewing necessities, techniques, and terminology. We learn to make quick pockets, button loops, and bag handles.

Chapter 2 is all about bags. You'll find fabulously fun and fresh bags that will make you want to sew.

Chapter 3 is about clothing. Make your everyday wardrobe exciting, fun, and new. You will learn to custom fit the clothing pieces at the beginning of the projects.

Chapter 4 is about home. Make things to add sweetness to the place where you relax, have fun with family and friends, and create memories.

I want you to love sewing as much as I do. Let's start sewing, friend!

xx, abi

FABRIC

When my sisters and I go shopping for fabric, we can't help but run our fingers over the bolts of fabric as we walk past them. Nothing feels better than fabric.

I've used a wide range of fabric types for the projects in this book—quilting cotton, home decor, flannel, voile, even a little velveteen just because I love it. I used quilting cottons most frequently and heavier home decor cottons second most. I also used these two together in several projects and loved the results. If you ever thought that the two weights of fabric couldn't be used together, think again! They complement each other beautifully. I made a versatile It's a Cinch Belt (page 86) by pairing them. When I want more texture, I wear it with the thicker, home decor fabric facing out; when I want a simpler, smoother look, I wear it with the lighter-weight side facing out.

I used flannel and corduroy to add texture to the patchy projects—such as the Memory Quilt (page 121) and the Pieces and Letters Pillowcase (page 116). To create clothing that hangs nicely on the body, I used buttery and lightweight voile and rayon. Both are a lot easier to sew with than many people think. I loved using a flowing voile for the Riverwalk Skirt (page 92) and rayon for the Party Frock (page 68).

I want you to feel free to play around with fabrics and substitute one type for another to get different effects, but it's also important to know a few things about the characteristics of fabric so that you aren't caught too off-guard by the results.

Fabric weight is very important to consider when choosing which fabric to use. Heavier fabrics are thicker and stiffer than lighter ones. This is great when you are making a tote bag but might not be good in a garment. If you want a skirt that gently blows in the wind, don't choose a stiff fabric that has a life of its own. You could end up looking like you are wearing a box instead!

People who sew often talk about the *drape* or the *hand* of fabric. You can check this by unrolling some from the bolt in the store and laying it across your hand. Does it stick out or drop down naturally? It will do the same thing on you.

I have recommended fabric weights in each project—either heavy, medium, or light. Often you have a choice of two weights.

Another way to think of fabric is by its content. I used cotton in nearly every project in the book, in all three weights. It's strong, breathable, and widely available in terrific prints. I used rayon in some of the clothing projects because it's also breathable and has great drape.

Choose the Right Fabric

Many of my bags and home projects call for home decor or heavyweight fabric. The fabrics I used are cotton home decor fabrics that come in a great range of colorful designs. Often soft canvas or sturdy twill home decor fabrics are not as thick as traditional upholstery fabrics and are much easier to use. They have enough strength and body to make great bags.

When a pattern calls for a midweight fabric, look no further than typical quilting cotton (sometimes called *calico*). Usually filling many aisles at a fabric store, these prints and solids come in a rainbow of colors. Flannels and corduroy are in this category, too, and their texture can be a welcome addition to many of the projects in this book. For even more fuzz, consider velveteen, a personal favorite of mine.

For skirts and some of the other clothing projects I recommend using lightweight fabrics. These include cotton voile and also rayons, which tend to have great drape. These thinner fabrics also are great as accent fabrics on projects that require something sturdier for the main pieces. Remember your voile scraps, for example, when covering a button or making a Loopie Loop (page 24). Lighter-weight fabrics handle curves the best!

Washing Your Fabric

I suggest not washing your fabric before you get started on a bag or home project. However, I do suggest prewashing, drying, and pressing fabric that will be made into clothes because you don't want them to shrink after you have sewn them. Wash your belt fabrics if you're going to wash your belt after wearing it a time or two.

If you're afraid something might shrink too much, wash it in cold water and dry it on low before you've made the project. If you pulled fabric from an available stash (your own, a friend's, your sister's) for one of these projects and it's already been washed, that's perfectly OK. Press the fabric well before you get started, and you'll be good to go.

Yardage

I would much rather you end up with a little extra fabric than discover that you don't have enough, so the yardage requirements are on the generous side. I also wanted to include enough in case the fabric has a one-way design. After all, a little leftover fabric in your stash can't hurt. But I still recommend using your fabric sparingly.

Please keep in mind that fabric width matters when calculating how many yards a project requires. When I mention a certain kind of fabric in the materials list, I'm assuming the standard width for that type of fabric:

- Quilting cotton and many woven apparel fabrics: 44″–45″

- Rayon and some other apparel fabrics: 58″–60″

- Home decor fabrics: 54″

- Interfacing: 20″

- Muslin: 36″–45″

The width of each fabric should be labeled on the end of the bolt or roll.

So if you decide to make a project out of quilting cotton instead of a suggested home decor fabric, you may need to add a half-yard or more to the suggested fabric requirements because quilting cottons usually come in narrower widths. You can lay out your pattern pieces on a table and estimate how much you'll need.

If you have wider fabric, you may need less. But it's always best to have extra fabric instead of running out!

If you prewashed your fabric, it may have shrunk a little bit, so check that your fabric is still wide enough to cut all your pieces as needed. I've assumed that your quilting cotton will still be at least 42″ wide after washing. The project instructions will tell you when you really need to check the width.

Puzzle It Out

Lay out all your pattern pieces on your fabric before cutting things out. That's correct! One of my problems is that I get excited and just start cutting away without thinking things through. But you are much more likely to end up without enough fabric that way. So, arrange the pattern pieces before cutting them out.

You will see that some projects use patterns in a pullout at the back of the book. You'll need to trace these so that you can use and reuse all of them. But many of the pieces you need to cut out are just given to you as measurements (for example, 2 pieces of fabric 14″ × 19″), not as drafted pattern pieces. If you're confident, you can use a wide, clear, gridded ruler (a quilter's ruler) to mark and cut these out directly from your fabric. I suggest making your own pattern pieces for these. Use a ruler and pen to draw the dimensions given on any large, lightweight paper. You can use freezer paper, kraft paper, the back of wrapping paper, or special pattern papers like Swedish tracing paper or red dot tracer paper (neither of these last two is actually paper, but is more like interfacing, which also works).

Making pattern pieces

Making your own pattern pieces is fun! It's work, but it's fun. Here's how I make last-almost-forever pattern pieces.

Start with your large paper. My favorite for making patterns is the red dot tracer paper, a nonwoven, somewhat transparent material that feels like interfacing and has small red dots in a 1″ grid. I like to use it because the red dots are terrific at helping you keep your lines straight and corners square, which is ideal when you're making pattern pieces

for projects such as the Amy bag, Belle bag, Party Frock, or Riverwalk Skirt. You can also stitch it, like Swedish tracing paper, and try it on when making and fitting garments. Red dot tracer paper practically lasts forever and is available at fabric shops and online.

When making pattern pieces, use a sharp pencil and long ruler to draw the dimensions directly onto the paper. Make sure any square corners are really square! A clear, gridded ruler, like a quilter's ruler, will help. Pay special attention to whether any of the pieces need to be cut on the fold, and if so, mark this on your pattern piece.

Cut the pattern pieces out and label them with the name of the project, the part, and the cutting instructions. For example:

Belle bag	**Maggie bag**
Side body	Handles

Place the pattern pieces in a labeled manila envelope so they won't be missing next time you want to sew!

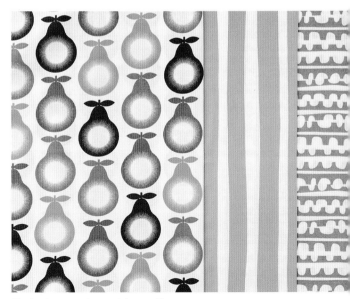

Cool colors together—violet + yellow-green

When putting fabrics together, think about what they'll be doing, what they'll be pairing with, and what part they'll play in your home or wardrobe. Naturally, you want your project to look good to you, so shoot for that first! Second, think about the color group—is it warm or is it cool?

Think about the size of print you're working with as well. Put a smaller print with a larger print. Choose a smaller print in a color that will draw out a favorite color in the large print. I did this throughout the book. For instance, I played off the background of the Memory Quilt (page 121) to choose the top pieces.

For thread, I suggest using matching threads for all the projects. However, thread and

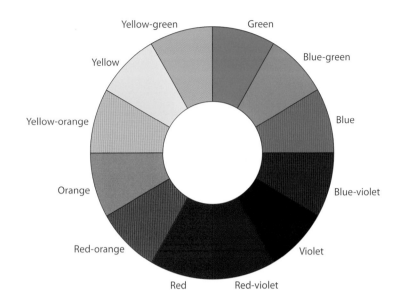

stitching can create pretty details. When you are comfortable with sewing and choosing colors, by all means, contrast thread colors with your fabrics!

Play with color. Don't let my choices throw you when you're playing around with your colors. I will have a slight idea in mind, and that's exactly what I go for—this creative inkling, this combination I think I will like.

Combine what you love and you'll always be pleased with the outcome! It'll work every time.

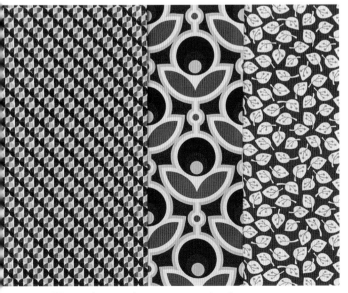

Warm colors together—orange + red-violet

Warm and cool colors together—red-orange + blue

MY SECRETS

Sewing Down Those Buttons

Sewing the buttons in place on any of these projects is a lot easier than one might think! Everyone has her own way of doing things, but I suggest using hand-quilting thread to sew on buttons. It's stronger and thicker than regular thread and will take the strain much better. It's even waxed to slide through the fabric. Keep a spool of it on hand, and you'll soon wonder how you ever got along without it!

Turning Things Out

Turning things right side out can be a challenge, no matter how developed your sewing skills are! I've tried very hard to avoid turning, but it's a necessity of sewing. Sometimes you just have to sew a narrow tube of fabric and turn it inside out to make a strap or a tie. I didn't want to leave you hanging if you came to a project (from this book or elsewhere) and didn't know the best way to do it.

I use the Turn-It-All (available at local fabric stores or online). This set of turners is a real treasure worth buying; I can't count how many times I've used it! However, if you don't have a special tool when you need something turned out, try your middle finger. Lick it lightly and use that to draw the fabric out from itself. If the hole is too small for your finger, use a bodkin (a small metal tool with a slit to hold a cord). Or use a chopstick or pencil to carefully poke out the corners.

You will see that on many of my projects I just fold the raw edges of the strap or tie to the center, fold it in half again, and sew it all together from the outside. I don't have to be concerned with turning the little sucker, and it looks fine for many projects.

SEW *clever!*

When you know before you even start that you'll have problems turning a strap or tie right side out, cut a piece of skinny ribbon or trim longer than the problem piece. Place the piece of ribbon at the end that will be sewn, and catch it in the seam allowance. When it's time to turn the tube right side out, use the ribbon to pull the tube right side out. Trim the ribbon close to the seam when you're done!

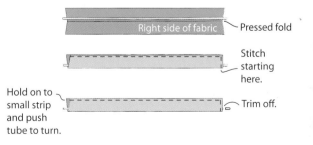

Right side of fabric — Pressed fold

Stitch starting here.

Hold on to small strip and push tube to turn. — Trim off.

Threading Things Through

I guess if you're a pro at sewing, you know what kind of thread you like to use on your machine. However, if this is your first sewing book and you are at a loss as to what thread you should purchase for that sewing machine of yours, try a strong and durable all-purpose thread such as Coats and Clark Dual Duty XP.

Surefire Gathering

Use cotton crochet thread and regular thread and the zigzag stitch on your sewing machine. Sew with the wrong side of the fabric facing up, and lay the crochet thread down where you are about to sew. Zigzag over it; then knot one end of the crochet thread when you're finished stitching, leaving a tail at the other end. Pull the tail to make the gathers. Pull the thread out after your gathered piece is sewn in place. **Figures A & B**

tip
Be careful to keep the crochet thread centered in the middle of the zigzag as you stitch. If the thread is caught in the sides of the zigzags, you won't be able to gather it up later.

Although using my surefire way to gather things (above) is my favorite go-to, I love falling back on another super-simple way to gather fabric. It's especially fabulous on buttery fabrics like cotton voile and rayon. As a matter of fact, I used this simple way to gather on every single tier of my Riverwalk Skirt (page 92)!

Turn your machine to the longest straight stitch possible (mine goes up to 5.0). Run two lines of straight stitches where you want to gather, just about ¼″ apart. Leave long thread tails at either end. Unlike most other stitches, you won't be backstitching at the beginning and end. Pull the thread tails to the desired amount of gathering and disperse the gathers evenly. Knot the thread tails and cut off any excess. After you've sewn the gathered piece in place, you can pull out the gathering threads. **Figures C & D**

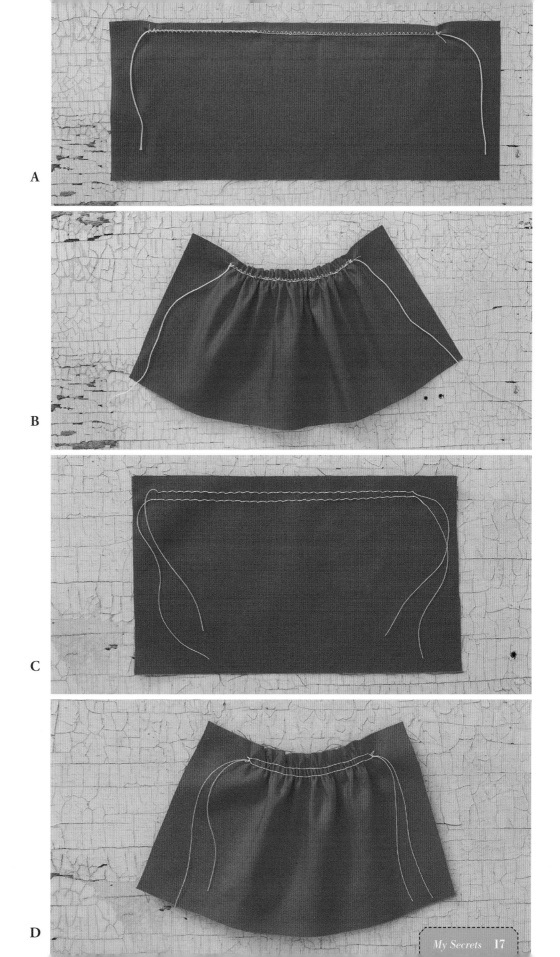

A

B

C

D

Go Ahead and Pin

Unlike most sewists, I don't really truly rely on pinning. I guess I just found that my projects came together faster when I didn't bother with pinning the pieces for every single seam together. I don't pin quilt blocks together. I don't pin when I'm sewing up a pocket or Loopie Loop. But I can't deny the fact that pins are fabulous, and I do, on special occasions, use them! (And bend them.) Pins keep your pieces, whatever they might be, from shifting and bubbling. In making the projects for this book, I used pins with the bags, (most of) the clothing, and when I put together the top pieces on the base blocks for the Memory Quilt. You can sew with or without them. But anytime you see some possible slippage or movement (like when you're using voile or rayon), pin. Pinning will make your sewing really sing. Just don't sew over your pins—this can hurt your needles, your machine, or you!

A Use for Leftovers

The thrilling news about being smart when buying and using fabric is that you can use your leftover scraps for other projects in this book! When cutting out any project, place your pattern pieces as close to one another as possible. Then use the scraps whenever you decide to make a Pieces and Letters Pillowcase (page 116) or a Betty Pouch (page 62).

Elastic Maneuvering

Safety pins have replaced my bodkin for pulling elastic through waistbands. Attach the safety pin to the elastic, and then wiggle it through the opening, pulling the elastic behind it. I use large and small pins, depending on the project or the waistband.

By Hand?

I love doing hand quilting. It's handwork that can travel with you. One of my favorite hand-quilting designs is a simple fan pattern that I made up. It has the look of a rainbow and is super simple to make, even for a beginning quilter! I use perle cotton thread to make my stitches really sing and show up on my quilt. Perle cotton thread is fun to work with, too. Keep some of this thread on hand so you can pull it out next time you have a quilt that's begging to be quilted by hand—this time, anyway!

Slip stitch

Slip stitches are the way to go when you need to sew an opening or seam closed by hand and don't want your stitches to show.

Try this when you are finishing the binding around a quilt. You will be working from the back of the quilt. Fold the binding over from the front so it hides the machine stitching. Thread your needle with about 18″ of thread, knotted at one end. Take your first stitch through just the backing and the batting, hiding the knot where it will be covered by the binding. Then put your needle through the folded edge of the binding, directly opposite where it comes out of the back of the quilt.

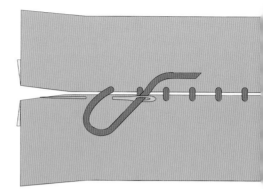

Run the needle inside the binding a short bit, bring it out, and stitch directly into the backing the same distance. Keep on slipstitching till the binding or opening is all stitched.

The goal when you slipstitch is to make sure that your stitches aren't visible on the quilt top. If you don't see your stitches—hooray!—it's perfect. If you see your stitches on the quilt top, you're bringing your needle through all the layers; you want to bring your needle through only the quilt back. Practice makes perfect. You can also slipstitch the turning holes in your purse linings for a neat finish.

SEW *clever!*

Just some things I've learned:

- *Tired of your plain leggings? Add three or four small mother-of-pearl buttons in a row down the outside of each leg!*

- *Have an old cardigan that needs a little pop? Remove the old buttons and replace them with sweet mother-of-pearl buttons or some fun, colorful buttons.*

- *Having trouble removing stains? Try using Ivory liquid soap. Lightly rub some onto the stain and throw the item into the washer. It's amazing at removing stains and spots.*

- *Need a storage idea for buttons? Store your vintage and new buttons alike in clear glass Ball jars. Not only will this keep your buttons easily accessible, but they look really fun and pretty on your crafting table or studio shelf!*

NECESSITIES

I consider certain things necessities for a good, happy sewing table:

A good sewing machine. I love Janome! The first sewing machine I ever owned was a Janome Jem Gold. They're smaller than other machines but considerably heavy-duty for their size. You can purchase them on eBay for very reasonable prices.

A good pair of scissors. I have a soft spot for Fiskars brand.

A good pair of pinking shears. The zigzag blade is one of my very favorite ways to finish off seams so they won't fray.

A little pair of scissors (snips). Great for sitting right by your machine or to have on the arm of the couch while you're hand quilting or doing any kind of handwork.

A seam ripper. It's my best friend and will be yours too.

Needles. Hand sewing is relaxing, so I do it a lot! I keep all types and all sizes of needles in my pincushion. For hand quilting on quilts (when I'm using cotton crochet thread), I use a larger needle with a long eye. When I'm sewing on buttons, I use smaller needles. I buy the assorted pack, which includes long ones and short ones with big eyes and small eyes, and they all seem sharp to me!

Measuring tape. I use my measuring tape for everything.

Straight pins. Good, colorful pins. (I'm sorry that I'm constantly bending you.)

A seam gauge. I love you. The absolute best for marking hems, waistbands, pocket placements, whatever!

Safety pins. See Elastic Maneuvering (page 18). Amazing little things. Time and money savers.

A bodkin. I hardly ever use it since I discovered the amazing safety pin, but I still suggest having one on hand.

A small notepad, pencil, pen, chalk markers, and disappearing-ink markers. For marking darts, marking where to start sewing and where to stop, jotting down notes, and other tasks, they all can play an important part in your sewing adventures. Make sure you test any disappearing-ink markers on your fabric first.

An iron. It will be your best friend in making your project turn out just beautifully. Press after every seam for the best results. Crisp and clean!

A spray bottle with water. I use one all the time to dampen seams when pressing them open and to help press the wrinkles out. Water is better for your fabric than spray starch and doesn't leave any scent!

A cutting board; rotary cutter; and clear, gridded ruler. These items will make your sewing project a lot more enjoyable. They will keep you on a straight path and can be helpful when measuring and drawing out your own pattern pieces.

THINGS YOU'LL NEED TO KNOW

Some Techniques

Pockets

I've made all the pockets in this book exactly the same way—they are all patch pockets. The sizes may vary, but the method does not.

1. Look for the pocket size in the project directions. Cut out the square or rectangle in the size given.

2. Fold the pocket piece right sides together through the width (so a long rectangle would become a shorter rectangle or a square). Stitch along the left and right sides with a ½″ seam allowance, leaving the side parallel to the fold open. Trim the corners and turn right side out. Press. **Figure A**

3. Zigzag or serge the opening closed. This is now the bottom of the pocket. **Figure B**

4. Follow the project directions for where to place the pocket. As for how to place the pocket, put it bottom edge up, right sides together—the right side of the pocket against the right side of the bag, bag lining (if it's an inside pocket), or other project. Pin it in place so it stays straight and even.

note The pocket does not get placed where it will be when it is finished. Rather, the bottom of the pocket is on the bottom placement line, with the pocket hanging down. When it's flipped up, it lands in the right place.

5. Sew along the bottom edge of the pocket with a ½″ seam allowance. **Figure C**

6. Flip the pocket up along the bottom seam so that the front side is now visible. Your zigzag stitches should be hidden, and the pocket should be lying flat.

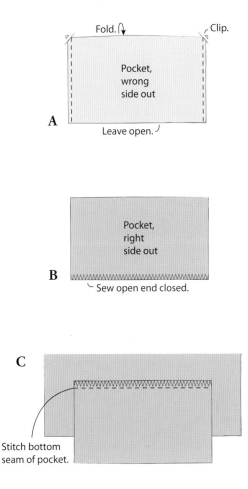

A — Fold. / Clip. / Pocket, wrong side out / Leave open.

B — Pocket, right side out / Sew open end closed.

C — Stitch bottom seam of pocket.

7. Pin and sew both sides close to the edges, leaving the top open. That's a finished pocket. **Figure D**

8. Sew down the middle of the pocket to make 2 smaller pockets if the directions tell you to (or if you prefer). **Figure E**

Loopie Loops

I've included button loops on several of these projects. Almost nothing can finish off a bag like a cute button (sometimes covered, sometimes not) and button loop. Less intimidating than a zipper or snap, my button loops are all made the same way—simple and fast.

Find the loop measurements for the project you're making.

1. Fold and press the strip in half lengthwise, wrong sides together. Open it up, fold the raw edges in to the center on the wrong side, and press again. **Figure F**

note Raw edges are just the unsewn sides.

2. Fold the strip back along the original crease, so that the raw edges are hidden. **Figure G**

3. Stitch along both long sides ⅛″ (or less, if you're a pro) from the edges. **Figure H**

4. Fold the stitched loop in half and press it in the shape of a slightly pointed U, with the folded side of the loop facing in. Make sure the raw ends are even. Place as directed in the project. **Figure I**

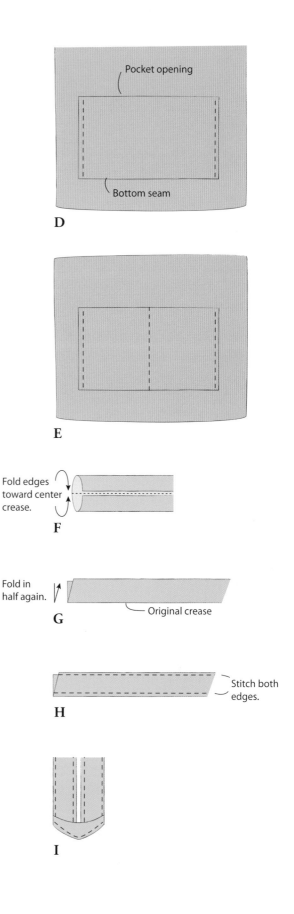

D — Pocket opening / Bottom seam

E

F — Fold edges toward center crease.

G — Fold in half again. / Original crease

H — Stitch both edges.

I

Handles and straps

Some of these are made with interfacing, and some are not. But they're all constructed the same way—and you won't have to dread turning them right side out!

Look for the width and length for the handle or strap in the project you are making, and cut the fabric to size.

Fusible interfacing is narrower than most fabrics, so you'll need enough to cut some pieces lengthwise, but you can use the remaining interfacing for other projects.

1. If the directions call for interfacing (or you are using lightweight fabric), follow the package instructions to fuse it to the wrong side of the fabric.

2. Fold, press, and edgestitch the strip(s) the same as for Loopie Loops (Steps 1–3, page 24).

3. Follow the project directions to place and attach the handle(s) or straps.

Some Terms

Box pleat: A pleat is fabric folded upon itself and partially stitched closed. Pleats are used to add dimension and detail. The box pleat is used to make the KittyJo bag (page 56) slimmer at the top, so it fits comfortably under your arm, but still keep its wide middle and bottom for plenty of storage. It also makes the bag a favorite with its fun and unusual look.

Gussets: Gussets are inserted pieces of fabric placed in the seams; in garments, they are often triangular. I use rectangular gussets at the bottom and sides of the Belle bag to add depth. Gussets are surprisingly easy to make and really handy to have in any bag!

Boxed corners: If you want a bag with depth but don't want to add gussets in the seams, you'll box the corners. You will make boxed corners on the Maggie bag (page 28), the Mia bag (page 38), and the KittyJo bag (page 56).

Yoke: A yoke, in a garment, is a piece of fabric across the top. On a skirt, it's the topmost section from the waist to the hips. In a blouse, it runs across the shoulders on the front and/or back. It frames your gorgeous face beautifully and is easy to sew. It also adds a little extra fun to your top. You'll make a yoke on view B of the Turnabout Blouse (page 98).

Narrow hem: The purpose of a narrow hem is not only to have no raw edges visible but also to take as little as possible from your garment. It is made by turning up about ⅛" of fabric at the edge or bottom of a garment, pressing it in place, turning up and pressing another ⅛", and machine stitching close to the edge. Some sewing machines have a special foot to help you stitch. You will use the narrow hem on the sleeves of the Turnabout Blouse (page 98).

CHAPTER 2: *bags*

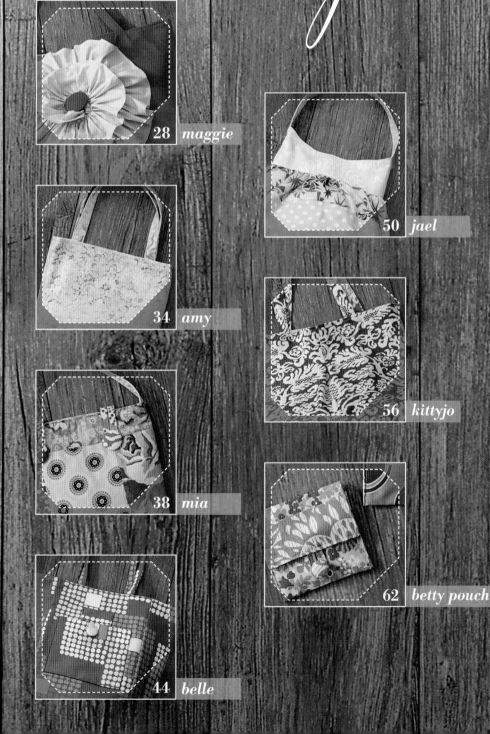

28 | *maggie*

34 | *amy*

38 | *mia*

44 | *belle*

50 | *jael*

56 | *kittyjo*

62 | *betty pouch*

SEW *clever!*

Having trouble remembering which is up and which is down on a pattern piece that's just about square? That happens to the best of us. I like to stick a straight pin into my fabric to mark the top. It makes things much less confusing and helps keep the project moving along since I don't have to stop and measure or drag out my paper pattern pieces to compare them to the cut fabric.

MAGGIE

FINISHED SIZE: 19½″ wide × 14½″ high × 5″ deep

Big, roomy, and floppy, the Maggie bag will be your best friend on a beach trip or any occasion. With a fun, large, happy flower on the front, Maggie won't just carry all your things—she'll also bring you a lot of compliments!

what you'll need

- Cotton fabric for exterior and straps: 1¼ yards

- Cotton fabric for lining: 1¼ yards (including pockets)

- Fusible interfacing, 20″ wide: 2½ yards

- Batting, 45″ wide: ¾ yard

- Cotton fabric for contrasting floppy flower: ⅝ yard

- Cotton crochet thread

- 1 button, 2½″ in diameter

Make the Pattern

On whatever you are using for pattern paper, draw a rectangle 25½″ wide × 18″ high. The best type of ruler for this is a wide, clear, gridded one, so that you can make sure your corners are perfectly square.

Mark 1″ in from both corners along the bottom line, and then draw new, angled sides from the top corners to the 1″ marks. This is the overall size of the pattern piece, and you're almost done!
Figure A

This bag has boxed corners to give it depth without a separate side or bottom gusset, so next we need to adjust the pattern to remove the bulk and make it easy to sew the boxed corners. Use your wide, gridded ruler to draw 2⅝″ × 2⅝″ squares at the bottom corners. Just line up the 2⅝″ marks on your ruler with the side and bottom lines at a corner of your pattern. Trace the 2 inner edges of the ruler to draw the new corner. Repeat on the other side.

Cut the pattern out, cutting away the squares at the bottom corner as well. Label the pattern with the name, top, and bottom.
Figure B

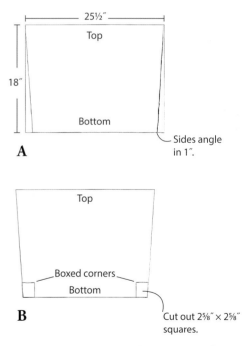

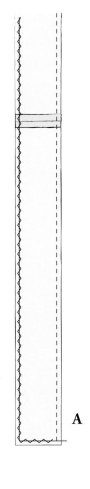

A

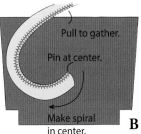

Pull to gather.

Pin at center.

Make spiral
in center. **B**

cut it out

- **Maggie pattern piece:** 2 exterior fabric, 2 lining fabric, 2 interfacing, 2 batting

- **For straps:** 2 pieces 4″ × 30½″

- **For pocket:** 2 pieces 15″ × 18½″

- **For flower:** 3 strips 6″ × 45″ (or the width of your fabric)

- **Interfacing for straps:** 2 pieces 4″ × 30½″

Putting It Together!

All seams are ½″ unless otherwise stated. Backstitch at the beginning and end of each seam and press the seams open.

1. Following the manufacturer's instructions, fuse interfacing to the wrong sides of the outer bag pieces. Baste a piece of batting to the wrong side of each of the lining pieces, all the way around the edge, using a ⅛″ seam allowance.

2. For the flower, sew the 6″-wide strips together at the short ends to create 1 long strip. Press the seams open. Sew a narrow hem (page 26) around all 4 sides. Use the method in Surefire Gathering (page 16) and cotton crochet thread to run a gathering stitch around 3 sides of the flower strip, right inside the hem, on the wrong side of the fabric. **Figure A**

3. In the center of the exterior bag front piece (just eyeball it), pin the end of the flower strip with the knotted crochet thread. Both pieces should be right side up. Pull on the thread to gather the strip, and coil it around the center point in a spiral. When you're happy with the look of your flower, pin it in place and sew it down on top of the zigzag stitch, either by machine or by hand. Make sure not to catch the ruffles as you stitch. **Figure B**

Optional step: Hand sew a button in the center of the flower. You can even cover a button in the bag fabric as I did. This is a fun embellishment, but your flower will look great without it too. Use strong thread to sew the button in place for a sturdy hold.

4. Sew together the outer bag front and back pieces, right sides together, along the sides and the bottom, but *not* the cut-out corner squares. **Figure C**

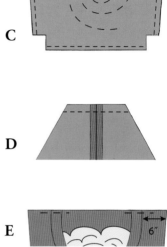

C

5. To box the corners of the bag, match up the bottom and side seams, so that the corner squares form straight lines. Sew along the raw edges on both sides. Turn the bag right side out. **Figure D**

D

6. Make the straps (page 25).

7. On each side of the exterior bag, pin a strap to the top, right sides together and matching the raw edges, 6″ in from the sides. Sew the straps down securely ¼″ from the ends. **Figure E**

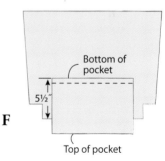

E

6″

8. Make the pockets (page 23).

9. On each bag lining piece, place the bottom of a pocket 5½″ up from the bottom of the lining and centered across the piece. Follow the rest of the instructions in Pockets (page 23) to attach the pockets. If you like, sew down the middle to create 2 smaller pockets. **Figures F & G**

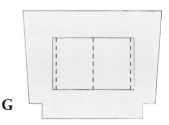

Bottom of pocket

5½″

F

Top of pocket

G

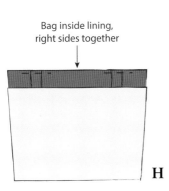

Bag inside lining,
right sides together

H

10. Repeat Steps 4 and 5 with the lining pieces, leaving a 6″ opening in the middle of the bottom for turning. You don't need to turn the lining right side out.

11. Fold the flower toward the center of the bag and temporarily pin in place. Place the bag exterior inside the lining, right sides together. Sew around the top of the bag with a ½″ seam allowance. **Figure H**

12. Pull the bag through the opening at the bottom of the lining. Unpin the flower, making sure that no part of the flower or bag got caught in the seam at the top of the bag. Push the seam allowances in the lining opening to the wrong side and sew it closed, either topstitching by machine or slipstitching by hand. Push the lining down back into the bag.

13. Topstitch around the top of the bag ¼″ from the edge.

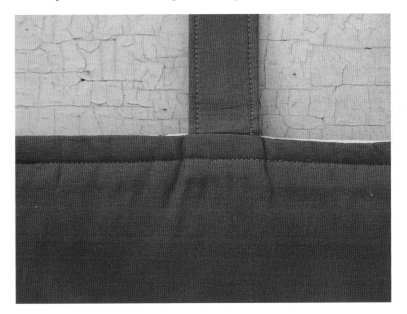

*Maggie is ready
for the beach!*

AMY

FINISHED SIZE: 12˝ wide × 13˝ high

The Amy bag was designed with magazines and books in mind. The handle length is perfect for hanging right at your side, and the width is suitable for several magazines and a good book. The pattern includes an optional inside pocket. Soon Amy will be tagging along with you everywhere.

SEW *clever!*

In this pattern the main pieces are almost square, so it's easy to get confused about which way is up. I place a straight pin at the top of each bag and lining piece. The top measures 13˝; the sides measure 14˝.

what you'll need

- **Home decor fabric:** ½ yard for bag exterior and handles

- **Lace fabric:** ½ yard for accent

- **Quilting-weight cotton fabric:** ⅔ yard for lining (including optional pocket) or ½ yard (if you are not making the pocket)

cut it out

- **Home decor fabric**

    For bag exterior: 2 pieces 13″ × 14″

    For handles: 2 pieces 4″ × 19″

- **Cotton fabric**

    For lining: 2 pieces 13″ × 14″

    For pocket (*optional*): 1 piece 8″ × 15″

- **Lace fabric**

    For bag front: 1 piece 13″ × 14″

Putting It Together!

All seams are ½″ unless otherwise stated. Backstitch at the beginning and end of each seam and press the seams open.

1. Make 2 handles (page 25).

2. Baste the lace piece to the bag exterior piece that you want to be the front, both right sides up.

3. At the top of an exterior bag piece, measure in 2½″ from each side. Pin the ends of the handle in place, matching the raw edges. Sew the handle down securely ¼″ from the ends. Repeat this step on the other exterior bag piece with the other handle. **Figure A**

4. Pin together the outer bag pieces, right sides together; sew the sides and bottom, leaving the top open. Trim the corners at an angle to reduce bulk. Turn the bag right side out. **Figure B**

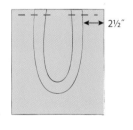

2½″

A

B

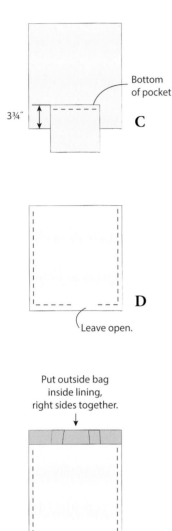

Bottom
of pocket

3¾″

C

Leave open.

D

Put outside bag
inside lining,
right sides together.

E

5. If you want to add a pocket to the bag lining, see Pockets (page 23) to make the pocket. Place the bottom of the pocket 3¾″ up from the bottom of the lining piece, centered from side to side. Follow the rest of the instructions in Pockets (page 23) to attach the pocket. **Figure C**

6. Pin the lining pieces right sides together. Stitch around the sides and bottom, pivoting at the bottom corners, and leaving a small opening in the middle of the bottom seam for turning. **Figure D**

7. Place the outer bag inside the lining, right sides together. Stitch all around the top. **Figure E**

8. Pull the exterior bag out through the opening in the lining. Fold the seam allowances in the opening to the wrong side and sew it closed, either topstitching by machine or slipstitching by hand. Push the lining down back into the bag.

9. Topstitch around the bag ¼″ from the top.

Load up Amy with all your good reads!

MIA

FINISHED SIZE:
9½″ wide × 13″ high × 3″ deep

The Mia bag is a real scrap buster—
it's the perfect way to use up miscella-
neous pieces of fabric that you love too
much to discard. Include up to twelve
different fabrics in this patchy bag and
take them wherever you go. With its
single cross-body strap, the Mia is a
terrific tote that's suitable as a book
bag or a purse.

what you'll need

- **Large scraps of midweight cotton, home decor, and/or voile fabric:** total of about 1 yard for bag exterior and straps

- **Midweight cotton fabric:** ½ yard (or more large scraps) for lining

- **Fusible interfacing, 20″ wide:** 1⅜ yards*

- **2 covered buttons:** 1½″ in diameter

Fusible interfacing is narrower than most fabrics, so you'll need enough to cut some pieces lengthwise, but you can still cut several more handles' worth of interfacing from this amount.

Make the Pattern

On whatever you are using for pattern paper, draw a rectangle 13½″ wide × 15½″ high. The best type of ruler for this is a wide, clear, gridded one, so that you can make sure your corners are perfectly square. Draw a horizontal line 3″ down from the top.

This bag has boxed corners to give it depth without a separate side or bottom gusset, so next we need to adjust the pattern to remove the bulk and make it easy to sew the boxed corners.

Draw a perfect square 1½″ × 1½″ at each bottom corner.

Cut the pattern out, cutting away the squares at the bottom corners as well. Label the pattern with the name, top, and bottom.

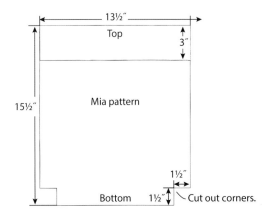

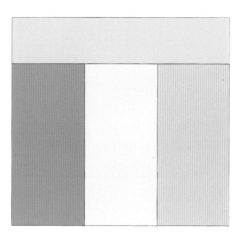

Patchwork Preparation

All seams are ½" unless otherwise stated. Backstitch at the beginning and end of each seam and press the seams open.

This scrappy style requires some precutting and sewing before you use your paper pattern.

From your scraps, cut:

- 2 pieces 4" × 17½" for the top of the bag exterior
- 6 pieces 6½" × 14" for the bag exterior

1. Sew 3 of the 6½" × 14" pieces, right sides together, along the long edges. Use a favorite fabric in the center, as the sides will be trimmed and not seen as much.

2. Sew a 4" × 17½" piece, right sides together, to the top of the patchwork sewn in the previous step.

3. Repeat Steps 1 and 2 to make the other side of the bag exterior.

cut it out

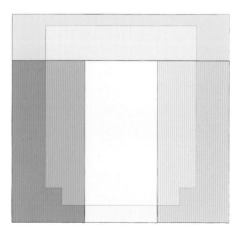

- **Mia pattern:** 2 lining, 2 batting, and 2 from your sewn patchwork pieces *(Place the 3" line on the pattern on the horizontal seam.)*

- **For strap:**

    1 piece 4" × 45" fusible interfacing (You can also cut 2 shorter strips across the width of the interfacing and butt them against each other when fusing to the strap.)

    1 piece 4" × 45" midweight cotton or home decor fabric (You can also cut this longer or shorter, depending on how you like your bag to hang. Use a measuring tape to find the right length.)

- **For button loops:** 2 pieces 2" × 9" midweight cotton or voile fabric

- **For pocket:** 1 piece 12" × 12" midweight cotton fabric

- **To cover buttons:** 2 fabric scraps 3" × 3"

Putting It Together!

All seams are ½" unless otherwise stated. Backstitch at the beginning and end of each seam and press the seams open.

1. Baste the pieces of batting to the wrong sides of the patchwork pieces ⅛" from the raw edges.

2. Cover the buttons according to the package instructions. Place the buttons on the front of the bag where the patchwork seams meet at a T. Sew the buttons on securely through both the bag and batting. (Use strong thread for a sturdy hold.) **Figure A**

3. Pin the patchwork bag pieces right sides together. Match the seam near the top. Sew along the sides and bottom of the bag. Don't sew the cut-out corners yet. **Figure B**

4. To box the corners of the bag, match up the bottom and side seams so that the corner squares form a straight line. Pin and sew along the raw edges on both sides. Turn the bag right side out.

5. Make button loops (see Loopie Loops, page 24). Pin the loops to the top of the back side of the bag, matching up the raw edges so the loops point down, right where the patchwork T's meet. Sew in place securely ¼" from the top of the bag. **Figure C**

A

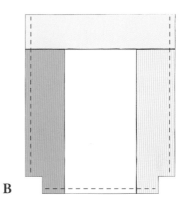

B

Back side

C

6. Fuse interfacing to the wrong side of the fabric for the strap. Make the strap (page 25). Pin the ends of the strap over the side seams of the bag, matching up the raw edges. Make sure the strap isn't twisted! Sew in place securely ¼" from the top of the bag. You might want to stitch back and forth across the strap a few times. The outer bag is finished! **Figure D**

7. Make a pocket (page 23). Pin the bottom of the pocket, centered, 5" up from the bottom of a lining piece, right sides together. Follow the rest of the instructions in Pockets (page 23) to attach the pocket. **Figure E**

8. Repeat Steps 3 and 4 to sew the lining pieces, leaving a 4" opening in the middle of the bottom seam.

9. Place the bag exterior inside the lining, right sides together. Sew around the top of the bag. Pull the exterior through the opening in the lining. **Figure F**

10. Fold the seam allowances in the lining opening to the wrong side and sew it closed, either topstitching by machine or slipstitching by hand. Push the lining down back into the bag.

11. Topstitch around the top of the bag ⅛" from the edge.

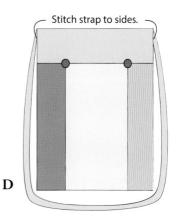

Stitch strap to sides.

D

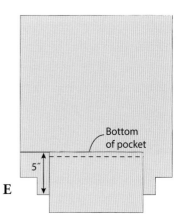

Bottom of pocket

5"

E

Put outside bag inside lining, right sides together.

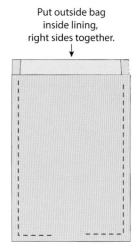

F

Put Mia on your shoulder and show off your favorite fabrics and scrappy style!

BELLE

FINISHED SIZE: 10˝ wide × 14˝ high × 7½˝ deep

Some days are super busy. Brunch with friends. Target shopping. Hitting a favorite flea market. Dance lessons. This is the bag to help conquer those long days. It's a perfect purse for big-bag lovers and can also be a great grocery tote. No matter what's inside, Belle looks swell!

what you'll need

- **Home décor fabric:** 1 yard for outer bag

- **Midweight cotton fabric:** 1 yard for lining and pocket

- **Batting, 45″ wide:** ⅝ yard

- **Canvas:** ⅝ yard for interlining

- **Fusible interfacing, 20″ wide:** 1 yard for handles*

- **1 covered button set:** 1⅛″ in diameter

Fusible interfacing is narrower than most fabrics, so you'll have to cut your pieces lengthwise, but you can still cut several more handles' worth of interfacing from this amount.

cut it out

- **For main body:** 6 pieces of fabric 11″ × 15″ (2 home decor for outside bag, 2 canvas for interlining, 2 midweight cotton for lining)

- **For bottom/side gusset:** 3 pieces of fabric 8½″ × 39″ (1 home decor for outside bag, 1 canvas for lining, 1 midweight cotton for lining)

- **For outside front pocket:** 1 piece home decor fabric 8½″ × 13½″

- **For handles:** 2 pieces home decor fabric 3″ × 28″

- **For button loop placket:** 1 piece home decor fabric 4″ × 4″

- **For button loop:** 1 piece midweight cotton or home decor fabric 2″ × 4½″

- **For inside pocket:** 1 piece midweight cotton fabric 10½″ × 13½″

- **For main body:** 2 pieces of batting 11″ × 15″ and 1 piece of batting 8½″ × 39″

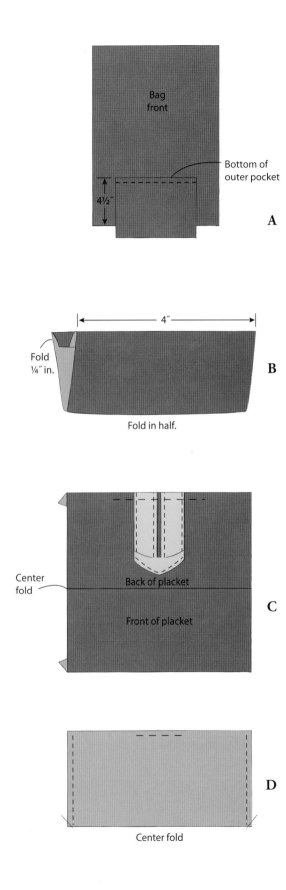

Bag front

Bottom of outer pocket

4½″

A

4″

Fold ¼″ in.

Fold in half.

B

Center fold

Back of placket

Front of placket

C

D

Center fold

Putting It Together!

All seams are ½″ unless otherwise stated. Backstitch at the beginning and end of each seam and press the seams open.

1. Baste the canvas pieces to the wrong sides of the matching home decor pieces. Baste the batting pieces to the wrong sides of the cotton lining pieces.

2. Make the front pocket (see Pockets, page 23). Sew the bottom of the pocket 4½″ from the bottom of an 11″ × 15″ home decor piece that you want to be the bag front. Follow the rest of the instructions in Pockets (page 23) to attach the pocket. **Figure A**

3. Make a button loop (see Loopie Loops, page 24).

4. For easier stitching later, fold and press the 4″ × 4″ square for the button loop placket in half. Then fold and press the long edges in ¼″ to the wrong side. Open up the folded square and place the button loop as shown, right sides together, centered on the long side that you want to be the back of the placket, and matching the raw edges. Baste the loop in place ⅛″ from the raw ends. **Figures B & C**

5. Fold the placket in half again, right sides together. Pin and stitch along the 2 short sides of the placket with a ¼″ seam allowance. Trim the corners and turn right side out. Tuck the raw edges of the unsewn side in along the fold line, flipping the button loop out. **Figure D**

6. Pin the placket with the loop pointing down, directly above and centered on the finished outer bag pocket. Edgestitch around all 4 sides of the placket to attach it to the front of the bag. **Figure E**

7. Cover the button, following the instructions on the package. Mark the button placement on the outer bag placket through the button loop. Using sturdy thread, sew the button to the pocket only—not to the bag!

8. Pin the home decor gusset piece to the remaining 11″ × 15″ home decor piece (this will be the back of your bag), right sides together, starting at the top right corner and working your way down the side, across the bottom, and back up the other side. Stitch together, pivoting at the corners. Clip the gusset seam allowance at the bottom corners if needed. **Figure F**

9. Repeat the previous step to sew the bag front piece to the other side of the gusset. Carefully clip all 4 corners at the base of the bag. Turn right side out. **Figure G**

10. Fuse the interfacing to the handle strips, following the manufacturer's instructions. Make the handles (page 25). Pin a handle to each side of the bag at the top edge, placing the ends of the handles in 2″ from the side seams. Sew each end in place with a ¼″ seam allowance. The outer bag is complete! **Figure H**

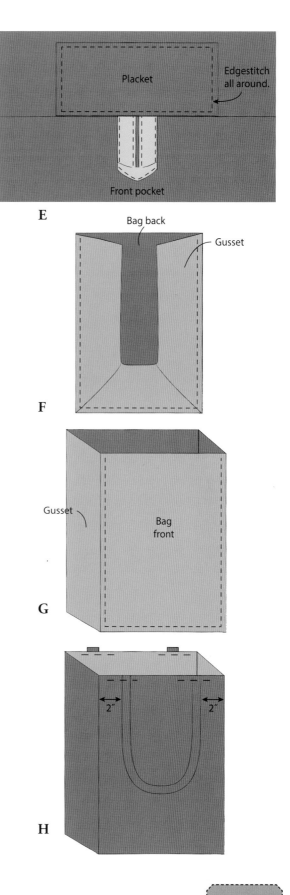

E

F

G

H

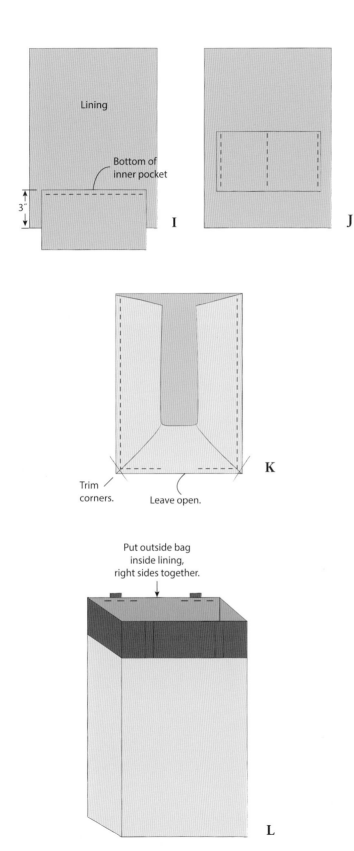

Lining

Bottom of
inner pocket

3″

I

J

Trim
corners.

Leave open.

K

Put outside bag
inside lining,
right sides together.

L

11. Make the inner pocket (see Pockets, page 23). Place the bottom of the pocket on an 11″ × 15″ lining piece, centered and 3″ up from the bottom of the lining. Follow the rest of the instructions in Pockets (page 23) to attach the pocket. Stitch a vertical line down the middle of the pocket to divide it into 2 sections. **Figures I & J**

12. Repeat Steps 8 and 9 to make the bag lining, leaving an opening in the gusset seam for turning. **Figure K**

13. Slip the outer bag into the lining, right sides together, matching the side seams. Stitch together all around the top. **Figure L**

14. Pull the outer bag out through the opening at the bottom of the lining. Check that you didn't catch any extra fabric at the top of the bag. Push the seam allowances in the lining opening to the wrong side and sew it closed, either top-stitching by machine or slipstitching by hand. Push the lining down back into the bag.

15. Topstitch around the top of the bag ¼″ from the edge.

Now you and your Belle are ready for every errand!

JAEL

FINISHED SIZE:
10˝ wide × 14˝ high × 10˝ deep

The Jael bag is a reversible bag that's super simple to sew. Intimidated by pockets? The Jael is for you—it has no pockets. And it's two bags in one! What are you waiting for? Let's sew!

what you'll need

- **Jael pattern piece:** for bag top (pullout page P2)
- **Home decor fabric:** ½ yard for Jael pattern pieces, base, and strap
- **2 different quilting-weight cottons or cotton voiles:** ¼ yard each for outer bag
- **Quilting-weight cotton or cotton voile:** ⅓ yard for inner bag
- **Fusible interfacing, 20″ wide:** ½ yard

cut it out

- **Jael pattern piece:** 2 outer fabric, 2 inner fabric, 2 interfacing for bag top
- **For inner and outer bag base:** 2 pieces 11″ × 11″ home decor fabric
- **For strap:** 1 piece 4¾″ × 20″ home decor fabric
- **For outer bag body:** 2 strips 5½″ × 43″ cotton or voile fabric*
- **For inner bag body:** 1 piece 10″ × 43″ cotton or voile fabric*

*If you've prewashed your fabric for the outer and inner bag bodies and it's not quite 43″ across, that's OK. You just need a piece at least 41″ long to fit.

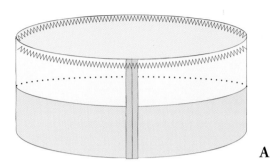

A

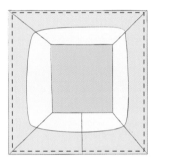

B

C

Putting It Together!

All seams are ½" unless otherwise stated. Backstitch at the beginning and end of each seam and press the seams open.

1. Sew the 5½" × 43" outer bag pieces right sides together along a long edge.

2. On whatever long edge you want to be the top of the bag, run a line of gathering stitches (see Surefire Gathering, page 16).

3. Sew the short ends of the outer bag piece right sides together to make a loop. **Figure A**

4. Pin and sew the bottom edge of the outer bag body to an 11" × 11" base piece, right sides together, matching the bag body seam with the center of a side. If needed, cut a slit in the seam allowance of the bag body at each corner as needed so it will turn the corners easily. Trim the corners at an angle to reduce bulk. **Figure B**

5. Following the manufacturer's instructions, fuse interfacing to 2 of the bag top pieces. Match up the pieces, right sides together, and sew along the 2 short sides to make a loop with a curved top edge. **Figure C**

6. Pin to mark the gathered edge of the outer bag body in quarters. Mark the centers (between the side seams) on the bag top. Pin the bag top along its straight edge to the gathered edge of the outer bag body, right sides together. Match the side seam of the outer bag body with 1 center pin on the bag top, and then match the remaining pins and seams. Pull on the gathering thread to gather the bag body to fit the bag top, adjust the gathers evenly around the bag, and pin the rest of the way. Stitch together and remove the gathering threads. **Figure D**

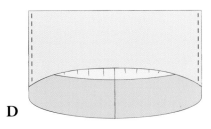

D

7. Make the strap (page 25). Pin the strap ends to the right side of the outer bag at the top, lining up the raw edges and strap ends over the side seams. Sew in place securely ¼″ from the upper edge of the bag top. **Figure E**

8. Repeat Steps 2 and 3 with the 10¼″ × 43″ inner bag piece.

9. Repeat Step 4 to sew the inner bag body to the remaining 11″ × 11″ base piece, leaving a small opening in the seam on a side for turning. **Figure F**

Stitch strap ends over side seams.

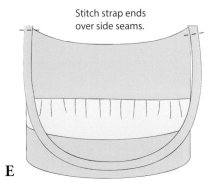

E

Leave open.

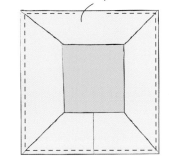

F

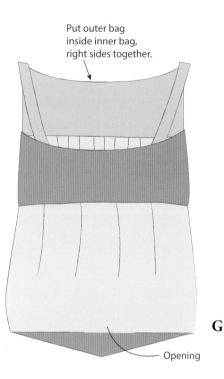

Put outer bag inside inner bag, right sides together.

Opening

G

10. Repeat Step 5 to sew the 2 remaining unfused bag top pieces together.

11. Repeat Step 6 to sew the inner bag body to the unfused bag top, right sides together.

12. Place the outer bag inside the inner bag, right sides together. Sew all around the top of the bag, following the curve of the pattern pieces. Carefully clip the seam allowance in the curved areas. Pull the bag right side out through the opening in the inner bag. **Figure G**

13. Push the seam allowances in the opening to the wrong side and sew it closed, preferably slip-stitching by hand since the bag is reversible. Push the inner bag back down into the outer bag.

14. Topstitch around the top of the bag ⅛″ from the edge.

Jael is two-sided, not two-faced— she's a good friend!

KITTYJO

FINISHED SIZE: 14½″ wide × 16¼″ high × 6½″ deep

This is a bag's bag! Large and roomy, this bag is perfect for housing lots of those little (and sometimes not-so-little) items. The pleat on the front adds detail, and the large boxed corners add space. Ballet flats will fit nicely in the bottom of the bag. And if you make the pockets just right, you can carry around someone's soda bottle, just for him, because he always asks. The KittyJo bag is not only cute but also sturdy enough to weather those long and rough days.

what you'll need

- **Home décor fabric:** 1 yard for outer bag and handles
- **Fusible interfacing, 20" wide:** 2 yards for outer bag and handles
- **Canvas:** ⅔ yard for bag interlining
- **Light- or medium-weight cotton:** 1¼ yards for lining and pocket

Make the Patterns

On whatever you are using for pattern paper, draw a rectangle 22" wide × 20½" high. The best type of ruler for this is a wide, clear, gridded one, so that you can make sure your corners are perfectly square.

Along the top 22" edge, draw vertical lines 10" in from either side and 5" down from the top. Label each of these lines *Pleat line*.

This bag has boxed corners to give it depth without a separate side or bottom gusset, so next we need to adjust the pattern to remove the bulk and make it easy to sew the boxed corners. Draw a perfect 3¼" × 3¼" square at each bottom corner.

Cut the pattern out, cutting away the squares at the bottom corners as well. Label the pattern piece *KittyJo outer bag* and mark the top edge. **Figure A**

To make the lining pattern, fold and pin (or tape temporarily) the outer bag pattern piece along the center pleat lines. Flatten out the pattern piece as best as possible, and trace the adjusted pattern onto a new piece of pattern paper. The top and bottom should have a slight curve—draw this as smoothly and evenly as you can. Cut the pattern out, label it *KittyJo lining*, and mark the top edge. **Figure B**

tip
You can make the lining pattern as directed in this project—or skip ahead! Cut the KittyJo outer bag pieces, sew the pleat, and cut the lining using the pleated bag front as your pattern.

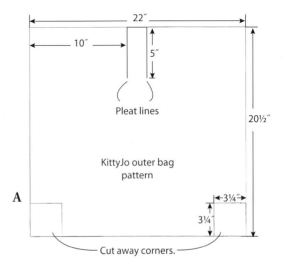

A

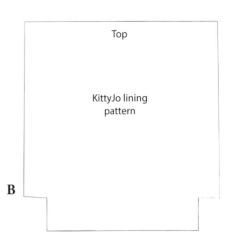

B

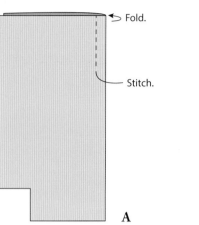

Fold.

Stitch.

A

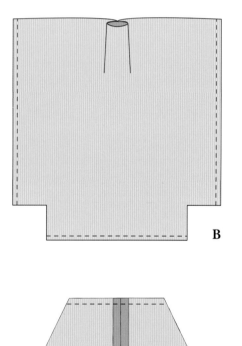

B

C

- **KittyJo outer bag pattern:** 2 outer fabric, 2 interfacing*

- **KittyJo lining pattern:** 2 inner fabric, 2 canvas

- **For pocket in lining** (*optional*): 1 piece of fabric 14½" × 18"

- **For outer fabric and interfacing for handles:** 2 rectangles 5" × 26" each

It's OK if your interfacing is a little narrower than your pattern piece. Just center the shorter side of the pattern piece across the width of the interfacing.

Putting It Together!

All seams are ½" unless otherwise stated. Backstitch at the beginning and end of each seam and press the seams open.

1. Follow the manufacturer's directions to fuse interfacing to the wrong sides of the outer bag pieces and the handles. (If you have a smaller interfacing piece, make sure to center it on the outer bag pieces. The areas without interfacing will be inside the seam allowances, which will work out just fine.) Baste the matching canvas pieces to the wrong sides of the lining pieces ⅛" from the raw edges.

2. Transfer the pleat line marks to the wrong sides of the outer bag pieces. Fold an outer bag piece right sides together, matching the lines. Pin; then stitch on the line through both layers. Press the pleat flat, centering it over the seam. Repeat with the remaining outer bag piece. **Figure A**

3. Sew together the outer bag front and back pieces, right sides together, along the sides and the bottom, but *not* the cut-out corner squares. **Figure B**

4. To box the corners of the outer bag, match up the bottom and side seams so that the corner squares form a straight line. Sew along the raw edges on both sides. Turn the bag right side out. **Figure C**

5. Make the handles (page 25). Don't forget to interface them. On each side of the exterior bag, pin a handle to the top, right sides together and matching the raw edges, 5″ in from the sides. Sew the straps down securely ¼″ from the ends. Your outer bag is finished! Set it aside. **Figure D**

6. Make the pocket (see Pockets, page 23). Place the bottom of the pocket 7″ up from the bottom of a lining piece, centered from side to side. Follow the rest of the instructions in Pockets (page 23) to attach the pocket. This is a wide pocket, so you may want to stitch a vertical line through the center to divide it in half. **Figure E**

7. Repeat Steps 3 and 4 with the lining pieces, leaving a 6″ opening in the middle of the bottom for turning.

8. Place the outer bag inside the lining, right sides together. Sew around the top of the bag. **Figure F**

9. Pull the outer bag through the opening at the bottom of the lining. Push the seam allowances in the lining opening to the wrong side and sew it closed, either topstitching by machine or slipstitching by hand. Push the lining down back into the bag.

10. Topstitch around the top of the bag ¼″ from the edge.

KittyJo will forgive you if you drop her willy-nilly after a tiring or exasperating day.

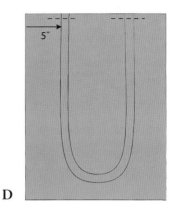

D

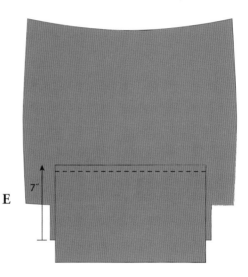

E

Put outside bag inside lining, right sides together.

F

SEW *clever!*

For an unusual and fun look, use two different fabrics or the same print in two different colors for the outside of the KittyJo bag! This makes an adorable bag even more adorable and so much fun to make and carry!

MICHELE'S D-RING IDEAL

This is a fun addition to any big bag! What I love about it most is that you can easily add it anytime you want. You've already finished the bag? Super. You've been carrying it for months? Dandy! Now you know you need this—the D-ring Ideal. Get a D-ring and a little piece of leftover fabric to make this adorable, handy addition. It's perfect for holding the car keys and the Betty Pouch (when made with the fun clasp) close to the top of your bag, so you don't have to go digging—and digging—for them when it's time to go or pay.

what you'll need

- 1 D-ring: 1½″ wide
- Scrap of quilting-weight cotton fabric
- Bag to sew it on!

cut it out

- 3″ × 3½″ piece of fabric

Putting It Together!

1. Take the 3″ × 3½″ piece of fabric and follow the instructions for the Loopie Loop technique, Steps 1 and 2 (page 24), to make a strip ¾″ wide × 3½″ long.

2. Fold the strip around the flat side of the D-ring, matching up the raw ends of the strip. Sew across the strip as close to the D-ring as possible. **Figure A**

3. Decide where you want to place the D-ring on the inside of your chosen bag. I suggest 1″–1½″ from the top.

4. Fold the raw ends of the strip to the inside and pin the strip in place inside your bag. Make sure the outside of the bag fabric is flat and smooth.

5. Sew in place around all 4 sides, and then sew an X in the middle. **Figure B**

Your Michele D-ring Ideal is finished! I'm going to use mine for my two keys and ridiculous number of key chains!

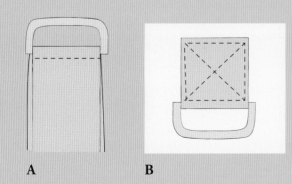

A   B

BETTY POUCH

FINISHED SIZE: 5″ × 4½″

This is a great beginner's choice! (And if you're not a beginner, make it with your favorite fabric scraps.) For change, cash, credit and gift cards, or maybe just odds and ends that would otherwise roll around the bottom of your bag, the Betty Pouch is a perfect fit. And its super-easy, quick construction just may have you making it for friends, too.

what you'll need

· **Fabric scraps:** of any weight or type

· **1 covered button set:** ⅞″ in diameter

cut it out

· **For main pouch exterior:** 1 piece of fabric 6″ × 8¾″

· **For pouch exterior:** 2 pieces of fabric 3¼″ × 6″

· **For pouch lining:** 1 piece of fabric 6″ × 13¼″

· **For button loop:** 1 piece of fabric 1½″ × 3½″

· **To cover button:** 1 square of fabric 3″ × 3″

Putting It Together!

All seams are ½″. Backstitch at the beginning and end of each seam. Press after sewing each seam.

1. Cover the button, following the instructions on the package. Set aside.

2. Make a button loop (see Loopie Loops, page 24).

3. To make the patchwork pouch exterior, sew the 3¼″ × 6″ pieces of fabric to the short ends of the 6″ × 8¾″ piece, right sides together. Press the seams open. **Figures A & B**

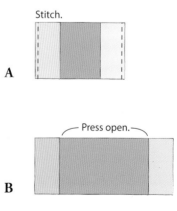

Stitch.

A

Press open.

B

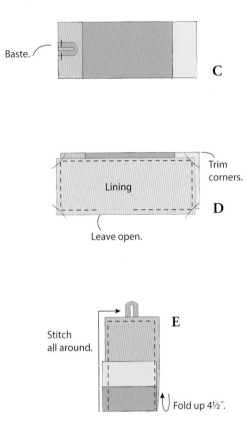

Baste.

C

Trim corners.

Lining

D

Leave open.

Stitch all around.

E

Fold up 4½".

4. Fold the button loop strip in half. Aligning the raw edges, pin the loop to the right side of the patchwork pouch exterior, centered on the end that you want to be the front flap of the pouch. Baste in place ¼" from the edge. **Figure C**

5. Pin and stitch the 6" × 13¼" lining piece, right sides together, to the exterior piece made in Step 3. Leave a small opening on a long side for turning. Trim the corners. Turn right side out and carefully poke the corners out. **Figure D**

6. Iron flat. Fold over the end without the loop 4½", lining sides together. Pin in place and topstitch all the way around, ⅛" from the edge. This will close up the sides of the pouch and put a nice finish on the edges. **Figure E**

7. Fold the flap down and place the covered button in the middle of the loop. Move the loop aside and stitch the button down firmly through the pouch front only.

Betty is ready to hold
your little treasures.

BETTY POUCH— CLASP STYLE!

The Betty Pouch is just as simple as before—only now you have a little easier access to it! Just perfect for hanging from Michele's D-ring Ideal (page 61) that you've put in your big bags.

- 1 swivel clasp
- Scrap of midweight cotton fabric
- Betty Pouch cut out

cut it out

- 1½″ × 3½″ piece of fabric for the clasp strap

Putting It Together!

1. Make another Loopie Loop (page 24) for the Betty Pouch. Fold and press it in half instead of a slightly pointed U.

2. Run the end of the clasp through the second Loopie Loop and pin the ends of the Loopie Loop together.

3. Sew the Betty Pouch exterior pieces together and add the button loop to an end, referring back to Betty Pouch, Steps 3 and 4 (pages 63 and 64).

4. Place the loop and clasp ⅝″ in from the short end opposite the button loop. Baste in place. **Figure A**

5. Refer back to Betty Pouch, Steps 5–7 (page 64) and continue to sew the Betty Pouch together as directed.

I'm pretty sure my keys, key chains, and Betty Pouch will hang out together on Michele's D-ring Ideal (page 61)!

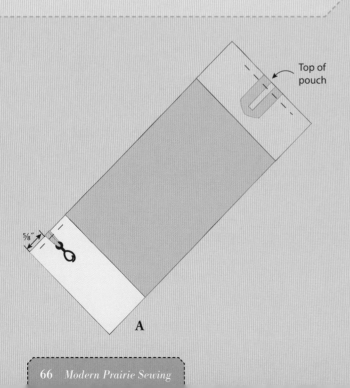

Top of pouch

⅝″

A

CHAPTER 3: *style*

PARTY FROCK

Sizes will vary—custom fit!

It's a party! You want to celebrate, enjoy, and feel comfortable. This is my favorite choice. But make every day and any day cute and comfortable—and even a celebration. This dress is not binding and has sweet gathered accents all the way around the top. Custom fit it without hassle. It can easily be lengthened or shortened—it can be a top, tunic, or sundress, all from one simple pattern. Knot the end of the straps and stitch them securely on the front for a special touch. The pattern includes an optional belt. Styling is entirely up to you, my friend.

what you'll need

- **Voile or midweight cotton fabric:** See Take Your Measure (below) and Cut It Out (page 70) to figure out how much fabric you need.

Take Your Measure

Wear leggings and a fitted camisole to get the most accurate measurements.

After you have all your measurements, you can make paper pattern pieces (see Making Pattern Pieces, page 12) and refer to Cut It Out (page 70) to figure out how much fabric you will need.

Measuring for your bodice bands

It's best to have a friend help with this.

1. Begin by measuring your high bust. To do this, wrap a measuring tape above your bust, just under your arms, and straight across your back. Hold the tape the way you want the bodice to fit—it shouldn't be snug or tight.

2. Divide your high bust measurement in half to account for side seams and then add 1¼″ for seam allowances. This is the cut length.

Example: Loose high bust measurement: 30″. Divide that number by 2 = 15″ + 1¼″ = 16¼″ long for each bodice band.

3. On your pattern paper, draw a rectangle 3¾″ × the cut length. Label it *Bodice band* and *Cut 4*.

Measuring for your shoulder straps

It's best to have a friend help with this.

1. Measure the distance as shown, from just under your shoulder blades, bringing the measuring tape straight over your shoulder and down to where you took your high bust measurement on your chest.

2. Add 2″ to this measurement to determine the cut length.

3. On your pattern paper, draw a rectangle 4″ × the cut length you determined in the previous step. Label it *Shoulder strap* and *Cut 2*.

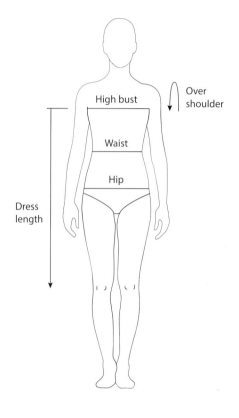

Measuring for your dress body

1. To determine the cut width of the dress body pieces, add 9″ to the cut length of your bodice bands.

Example: Band length 16¼″ + 9″ = 25¼″ cut width.

2. To determine the cut length of the dress body pieces, measure along your side from your high bust to where you want the party frock to hang on your body. To this number, subtract ⅜″ to account for the bodice band, hem, and seam allowances.

3. On your pattern paper, draw a rectangle the cut width × the cut length. Label it *Dress body* and *Cut 2*, and mark the top of the pattern piece.

cut it out

First you'll want to lay out your pattern pieces to figure out how much fabric you'll need. Don't forget to consider the width of the fabric you want to use. Also consider whether or not you need to place the pattern pieces so that the print goes in the same direction. Remember, you're cutting multiple pieces from each pattern piece.

Most likely, you'll need at least 2 times the cut length of your dress body plus an additional ½ yard. If you're skinny and your fabric is wide (wide enough to cut 2 dress body pieces across), you might need less.

Example: Cut length = 33″ for a long dress × 2 + 18″ (½ yard) = 84″ ÷ 36″ = 2.33, or 2⅓ yards needed.

You will need to cut the following pieces:

4 bodice bands (front, back, front facing, back facing)

2 shoulder straps

2 dress bodies

Pin your pattern pieces in place on the fabric. Make sure they are straight—measure how far the edges of the pattern piece are from the selvage to place the edge parallel. This is called placing the fabric on grain.

Cut out all the pieces.

Place a pin at the top of each dress body piece so the pieces don't get turned sideways.

Putting It Together!

All seams are ⅝″ unless otherwise stated. Backstitch at the beginning and end of each seam. Press the seams open after sewing.

1. Gather the top edge of your 2 dress body pieces (see Surefire Gathering, page 16). Set aside. **Figure A**

2. To make the shoulder straps, fold a strap piece in half lengthwise, right sides together. Stitch along the length with a ⅝″ seam allowance along the raw edges, pivot at the corner, and sew a short end closed, leaving the remaining short end open. Trim the corners, turn right side out, and press. Repeat for the remaining strap. Set aside. **Figure B**

3. To attach the straps, determine which of the bodice band pieces you want to be the back. Fold the band in half widthwise and mark the center at the top of the bodice band with a pin. Measure and mark 3″ out from the center. Pin the unstitched ends of the shoulder straps here, and baste in place ¼″ from the raw edges. **Figure C**

4. Pin and sew the bodice band facing pieces to the bodice bands, right sides together, along the long top edge of the bodice bands. On the back bodice band, the strap ends will be sandwiched between the 2 pieces. **Figures D & E**

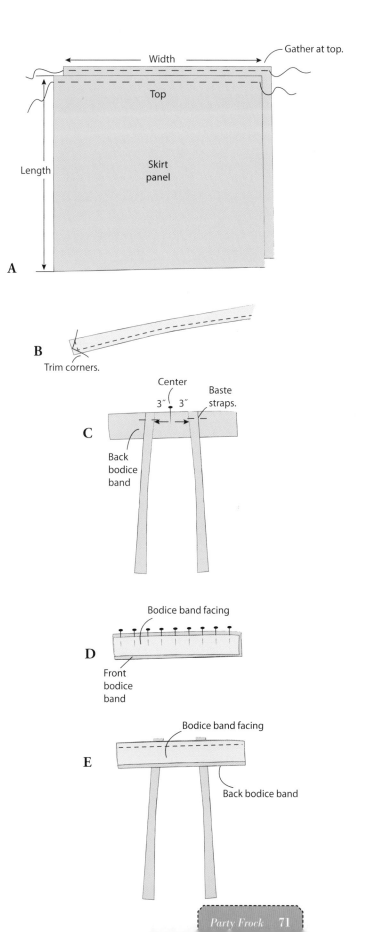

A — Gather at top. Width. Top. Length. Skirt panel.

B — Trim corners.

C — Center. 3″ 3″. Baste straps. Back bodice band.

D — Bodice band facing. Front bodice band.

E — Bodice band facing. Back bodice band.

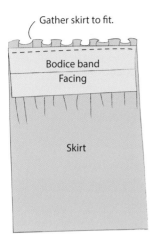

Gather skirt to fit.

Bodice band

Facing

Skirt

F

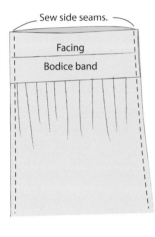

Sew side seams.

Facing

Bodice band

G

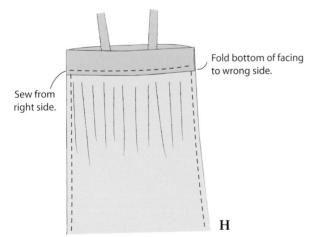

Sew from right side.

Fold bottom of facing to wrong side.

H

5. Pin the gathered edge of a dress body piece to the bottom of a bodice band as shown, right sides together, matching the raw edges at the sides. Pull the gathering thread on the dress body to adjust the gathers to fit evenly on the band. Pin all along the length of the band. Sew with the gathered side up, so you don't catch on the gathers as you stitch. Repeat with the remaining dress body and bodice band. Remove the long gathering threads. Press the seams toward the bodice bands. **Figure F**

6. Pin the dress front to the dress back, right sides together, matching the bodice seams. Knot the shoulder straps together and make sure to pull them away from the dress. Sew both side seams. (Be sure not to catch your straps!) Finish both side seams, starting right below the band seam, with pinking shears, zigzag stitching, or overlock (if you have a serger). **Figure G**

7. Fold and press the raw edge of the band facing ⅝" toward the wrong side. Fold the facing down inside the dress and press the top edge of the dress. Pin the folded edge of the facing in place, just covering the gathered bodice/dress seam. Topstitch through all the layers ⅛" from the seam. Press thoroughly. **Figure H**

tip

I get a better finished look if I pin the facing down from the right side of the dress and sew with the right side of the dress up on my machine.

8. Knot the ends of the straps, if desired. (Try the dress on to determine where to place the straps on the front and whether you need to adjust the knots.) Sew in place securely on the front bodice band. Try the dress on again to double-check the fit. If it's too loose around the bodice band, simply fold a couple of little tucks in the back of the band and stitch them closed by hand or machine. **Figure I**

9. To hem the dress, fold and press the bottom of the dress ¾″ to the wrong side, and fold and press ¾″ again so as to hide the raw edge. Hand or machine stitch close to the upper fold. **Figure J**

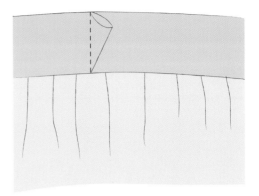

I

Now you're ready for a party, a holiday, or any day!

J

Fold.

SEW *clever!*

Make the Party Frock tunic length for a great swimsuit cover-up!

PARTY FROCK BELT

FINISHED SIZE: 1″ × approximately 88″

Here's an extremely simple version of a sweet belt that is designed to cinch up your Party Frock but can easily be worn with other dresses and clothes.

Putting It Together!

All seams are ⅝″ unless otherwise stated. Backstitch at the beginning and end of each seam. Press the seams open after sewing.

1. Sew the fabric strips, right sides together, at a short end. **Figure A**

2. Fold and press in half lengthwise, wrong sides together. Then fold and press both long edges in to the center crease. **Figure B**

3. Fold the short ends over ¼″ to the wrong side, and press. **Figure C**

4. Fold in half again lengthwise and topstitch all around the belt ⅛″ from the edge. **Figure D**

Your belt is ready to wear with anything now!

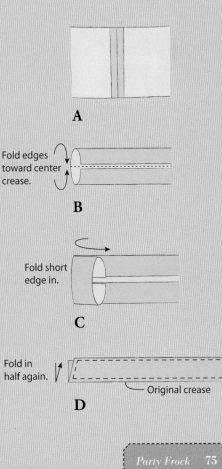

A

Fold edges toward center crease.

B

Fold short edge in.

C

Fold in half again.

Original crease

D

CAKEWALK SKIRT

Sizes will vary—custom fit!

This skirt is a breeze to make. Have fun mixing your choice of fabrics and prints. You can use up to six different fabrics, which can be challenging to coordinate but awfully exciting too. I loved going back and forth between two, three, or all six pieces cut from different fabrics. So easy to whip up, the Cakewalk Skirt is a pattern you'll come back to again and again. Traveling to an occasion a few hours away might find you traveling in a new skirt! Share the joy (and the cake) by making skirts for your friends too.

what you'll need

- **Cotton fabric:** amount will vary depending on your size (see Cut It Out, below) and number of fabrics used

- **Piece of elastic (2″ or 1½″ wide):** as long as your waist minus 1″

cut it out

Determine the dimensions of the 6 skirt pieces using the following formula:

1. Measure your waist and multiply that number by 2 (or 2.5 if you are especially curvy). Take that number and divide it by 6. (If your result is not a whole number, round up.) This will be the cut width of your pieces.

> *Example: Waist measures 27″ around: 27″ × 2 = 54″. 54″ ÷ 6 = 9″. The cut width for each piece would be 9″.*

2. The length of the 6 pieces depends on your height and how long you want the skirt. Measure (or ask a friend to do it) from your waist to where you want the skirt to end. Add 1½″ for a hem allowance. This will be the cut length of the 6 pieces.

3. Draw a rectangle on your pattern paper the cut width × the cut length.

4. Cut out 6 skirt pieces.

Putting It Together!

All seam allowances are ⅝″ unless otherwise stated. Backstitch at the beginning and end of each seam. Press the seams open after sewing.

1. Sew together 2 skirt pieces, right sides together, along 1 long edge. **Figure A**

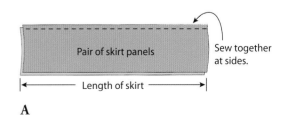

Pair of skirt panels

Sew together at sides.

Length of skirt

A

2. Repeat Step 1 until all of the pieces are sewn together into a big loop. Finish the seams with pinking shears, zigzag stitching, or overlock if you have a serger.

3. Run a gathering stitch around the top of your skirt ¼″ from the top. Use cotton crochet thread and a zigzag stitch (see Surefire Gathering, page 16) to make this easy. **Figure B**

4. Overlap the ends of the waistband elastic by about ½″, making sure it's not twisted. Zigzag stitch back and forth across the overlap several times for a secure hold. This will be the back of the waistband. **Figure C**

5. Decide what you want to be the front of your skirt. Fold it in half to mark the center front and center back with pins along the top; then fold in half again the other way to mark the top edge in quarters. Repeat this step to mark the waistband in quarters too.

6. Place the top edge of the skirt just inside the waistband, matching up the front, back, and side pins. Pull the gathering thread and adjust the skirt to fit inside the elastic. Use a zigzag stitch to sew the waistband to the skirt. **Figure D**

7. To hem your skirt, fold and press the bottom edge over ¾″ to the wrong side; then fold and press ¾″ again to encase the raw edge. Machine stitch the hem close to the upper fold. **Figure E**

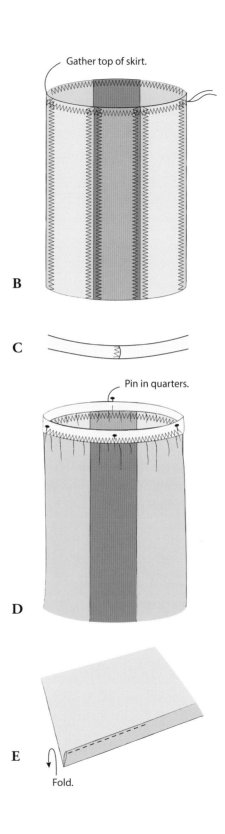

Gather top of skirt.

B

C

Pin in quarters.

D

E

Fold.

Isn't it cute? And wasn't that easy? A cakewalk!

SUNNY DAY SKIRT

Sizes will vary—custom fit!

The gathers here are unbelievably girly. The style is too adorable. But best of all? It works for everybody. It's as easy as pie to make and comes out right every single time. You can have it whatever length you like, whatever size you like. It'll definitely be a happy, sunny day!

- **Cotton, rayon, or voile:** See Take Your Measure (below) to determine yardage.

- **Piece of elastic (2″ or 2½″ wide):** cut 1″ shorter than your waist measurement

Take Your Measure

Measure (or get a friend to help you) from your waist down your side to the length you want your skirt to be. Add 2″ to that number to determine the cut length. Double that number and divide by 36 to determine how many yards to buy.

Example: You want the skirt to finish at 18″ long: 18″ + 2″ = 20″ × 2 = 40″ ÷ 36″ = 1.1, or 1⅛ yards. I usually want a little extra fabric for insurance, so I would buy 1¼ yards.

Cut 2 pieces the length you determined (see Take Your Measure, above) across the entire width of the fabric. If you're using a wider fabric, your skirt will be fuller than if it's made of 44″-wide fabric.

Putting It Together!

All seams are ⅝" unless otherwise stated. Backstitch at the beginning and end of your seams. Press the seams open after sewing.

1. Match up the 2 skirt pieces, right sides together, and sew along both selvage edges. Finish the seams with a zigzag or serge stitch. **Figure A**

2. Run a gathering stitch around your skirt ¼" down from the top. Use cotton crochet thread and a zigzag stitch (see Surefire Gathering, page 16) to make this easy. **Figure B**

3. Overlap the ends of the waistband elastic by about ½", making sure it's not twisted. Zigzag stitch back and forth across the overlap several times for a secure hold. This will be the back of the waistband. **Figure C**

4. Match up the side seams and fold your skirt in half to mark the center front and center back with pins along the top. Mark the waistband in quarters too.

5. Place the top edge of the skirt just inside the waistband, matching up the center front, center back, and side seams with the pins in the elastic. Pull the gathering thread until the skirt fits inside the elastic, adjusting the gathers evenly all around. Use lots and lots of pins to hold the gathers where they should be.

6. Sew a zigzag stitch around the bottom edge of the waistband, through the gathered top of the skirt. Make sure not to stretch the elastic as you sew. After the skirt is attached, stretch the elastic to test that the stitching holds. This also helps loosen up the gathers to make the skirt fit more comfortably. If the stitching breaks, don't worry—stitch it again. **Figure D**

7. To hem your skirt, fold and press the bottom edge over 1" to the wrong side; then fold over and press 1" again to encase the raw edge. Machine stitch the hem close to the upper fold. **Figure E**

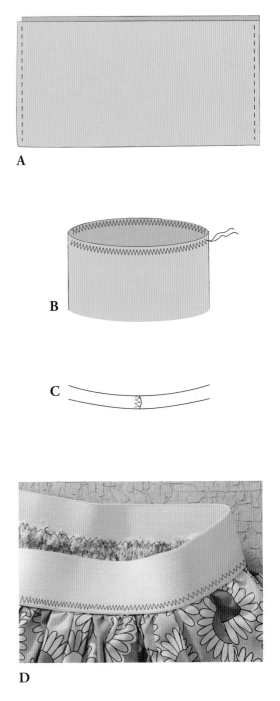

A

B

C

D

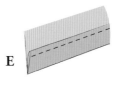

E

Now you've got a wardrobe staple that can bring sunshine even to cloudy or rainy days!

SIMPLE WRAP SCARF

FINISHED SIZE: 8″ wide; length will vary from 78″ to 118″, based on width of fabric used

The Simple Wrap Scarf is the ticket for keeping warm or adding a touch of panache. It's so quick to make that you'll find yourself making one to match every outfit you own. (Trust me.) Try making it out of voile, rayon, or even lightweight flannel or velveteen for a soft and cozy version to wear in the winter months. It works in many different fabric weights or even a combination of two.

- **Light- or midweight cotton, rayon, or linen (fabric A):** ⅝ yard

- **Contrasting light- or midweight cotton, rayon, or linen (fabric B):** ⅝ yard

- **Fabric A:** 2 strips 9″ × WOF*

- **Fabric B:** 2 strips 9″ × WOF

WOF = width of fabric

Putting It Together!

All seams are ½″ unless otherwise stated. Backstitch at the beginning and end of each seam. Press the seams open after sewing.

1. Sew together the fabric A strips along the short ends, right sides together. Repeat this step with the fabric B strips. **Figure A**

2. Pin together the A and B scarf pieces, right sides together, matching the seams and corners. Sew all around the outer edges, leaving an opening on a long side for turning. **Figure B**

3. Trim the corners and turn right side out. Gently push the corners out all the way. (Inserting a chopstick and carefully poking out the corners works wonderfully.) Press.

4. Slipstitch the opening closed, and then topstitch all around the scarf ¼″ from the edge.

A

B

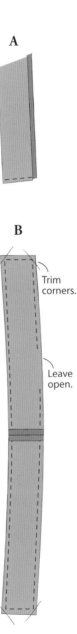

Trim corners.

Leave open.

Come on, chilly day, so I can wrap up in this cutie-pie scarf!

IT'S A CINCH BELT

FINISHED SIZE: 5˝ wide; length may vary from 78˝ to 118˝, based on width of fabric used

It takes hardly any time or fabric to make, but this belt is adorable when worn over practically anything, and it can be made reversible, too. Now, that's quite a belt! So cinch it up and be on your way. (Warning: Don't get tired of people asking you to make one for them, too. When you wear this belt, they'll come at a steady pace.)

what you'll need

- **It's a Cinch Belt pattern piece:** pullout page P2

- **Mid- or lightweight fabric:** ½ yard for main belt body and ties

- **Mid- or heavyweight fabric:** ⅓ yard for contrasting belt body

- **Fusible interfacing, 20″ wide:** ⅔ yard

cut it out

- **It's a Cinch Belt pattern:** 1 main fabric, 1 contrast fabric, 1 interfacing

- **For ties:** 2 pieces 4″ × WOF* of main fabric

WOF = width of fabric

Putting It Together!

All seams are ½″ unless otherwise stated. Backstitch at the beginning and end of each seam. Press the seams open after sewing.

1. To make the ties, fold and press a 4″ × WOF piece of fabric in half lengthwise, right sides together. Sew along a short end, pivot at the corner, and continue sewing all the way down the length of the tie, leaving the remaining short end open. Trim the corners. Turn right side out, poke out the corners carefully, and press thoroughly. Repeat this step with the remaining tie. Set aside. **Figure A**

2. Follow the manufacturer's instructions to fuse interfacing to the wrong side of the main fabric belt body.

3. Aligning the raw edges, pin the unstitched end of a tie to the right side of the main belt body as marked on the pattern piece. Repeat with the other tie on the opposite end of the belt. Fold the ties up in the middle of the belt and pin them in place, so they won't get in the way when you are sewing. Baste in place ¼″ from the ends. **Figure B**

4. Pin the main belt body to the contrast belt body, being careful to keep the ties out of the seamline. Sew around the belt, leaving an opening on a side of the belt for turning. Trim the corners and clip the curves. **Figure C**

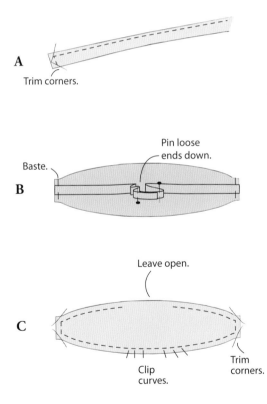

A Trim corners.

Baste. **B** Pin loose ends down.

C Leave open. Clip curves. Trim corners.

D

5. Turn the belt right side out. Unpin the ties in the middle and gently tug on them to help pull the belt right side out. Carefully poke out the corners and press thoroughly. Topstitch around the belt body ⅛″ from the edge. If you really love topstitching, though, do the long skinny ties, too! **Figure D**

Cinch up your belt and go!

FLOWER IN YOUR HAIR

FINISHED SIZE: 3˝ diameter

There's nothing more enjoyable than topping off an outfit or hairstyle with a cute little flower. This one looks perfectly at ease alongside a messy bun, above a braid, or holding back bangs that are growing out.

- **Cotton or voile fabric:** long scrap or ⅛ yard
- **Small scrap of canvas**
- **¾″ covered button set or regular button**
- **1½″-long metal barrette**

- **Cotton fabric**

  For flower:
  1½″ × 28″ strip

  To cover button:
  2″ × 2″ square

- **Canvas:** 3″ × 3″ square

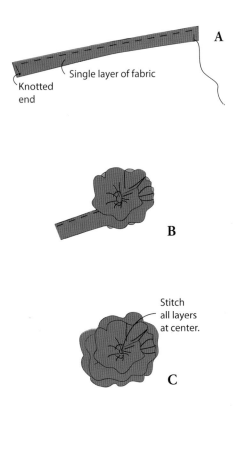

A

Single layer of fabric

Knotted end

B

Stitch all layers at center.

C

Putting It Together!

1. Cover the button, following the package directions or choose a regular button that would look good as the flower center.

2. Thread a hand-sewing needle with a long piece of thread. Knot your thread; bring the needle up from the wrong side of the fabric at a corner. Stitch a running stitch along the short end, pivot at the next corner, and stitch down the length and along the other short end. **Figure A**

note I tried gathering my strip using a long stitch on my sewing machine, but it looked much prettier when I did it by hand!

3. Pull the thread, and a flower shape will begin to appear quickly. Pull until the thread is tight, and coil the gathered strip in a pleasing flower shape until you like how it looks. Knot your thread and trim it off. **Figure B**

4. Stitch through all the layers at the center of the flower until the shape is secure. Knot your thread and trim it off. **Figure C**

5. Place the button in the center of the flower and sew in place. Knot and cut off the thread when the button is secure. Set aside. **Figure D**

6. Center the barrette on the square of canvas, with the top of the barrette facedown on the canvas. Open the barrette and stitch across it several times with sturdy thread. Trim the canvas around the barrette so that only a scant ½″ extends beyond the edges.

7. Hold the canvas side of the barrette against the back of the flower. Using small stitches, sew the canvas to the flower all around the edges. Grab as little as possible of the flower fabric with your needle. Some stitches may be seen, but that's OK! Make a strong knot at the end and trim off the thread. **Figure E**

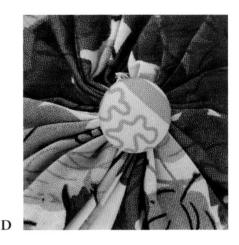

D

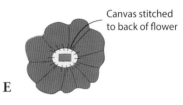

Canvas stitched to back of flower

E

Tuck this adorable flower into a messy bun. Gorgeous!

RIVERWALK SKIRT

Sizes will vary—custom fit!

This fun skirt takes more time and effort than the other two skirts in the book, but the end result is worth it! Make the Riverwalk Skirt out of a lightweight fabric with a nice drape, such as voile or rayon. What I love about this skirt pattern is that it actually has several different "views." It can be knee length or floor length, depending on the width you make the tiers. It's a favorite with my sisters and friends!

SEW *clever!*

It can be hard to tell which is the front and which is the back of a handmade skirt. Here's an at-a-glance way to mark the back. Fold a small length of ribbon in half and catch the raw edges of the ribbon in the casing as you sew the channel.

- **Voile, rayon, or other light-weight fabric:** See Take Your Measure (at right) to determine yardage.

- **Piece of elastic, ½″ wide:** 1″ shorter than your waist measurement

*Voile and rayon work best for the maxi length. (I needed approximately 5 yards of voile.) Midweight cottons as well as voile and rayon work for knee length.

Take Your Measure

It can be easier to have a friend help with some of these measurements. Mark them down because you'll need them to figure out the size to cut your pieces and how much fabric you'll need.

Yoke

The yoke is the fitted portion at the top of a garment. (In this case, it goes around your hips. It can also be the shoulder area of a top, like the Turnabout Blouse, page 98.)

Measure around your hips at their widest point and add 3″. This will be the length of the skirt yoke piece. The cut width of the yoke is 5″.

Example: Hips measure 40″, add 3″ = 43″. The cut size for the yoke would be 5″ × 43″. If your fabric isn't wide enough, you can also cut the yoke in 2 pieces and sew them together.

Determine the width of the tiers

Measure the distance from your waist to the floor for a maxi skirt (remember to account for the heel height of your shoes) or to the place you want your skirt to end.

From that number:

Subtract 3⅜″ for the finished yoke.

Divide by 5 and round to the nearest quarter inch.

Add 1¼″ to this for seam allowances to determine the cut width of each tier.

Example: Distance from waist to floor is 41″.

41″ − 3⅜″ = 37⅝″ ÷ 5 = 7.525″

In this case, round down to 7½″.

7½″ + 1¼″ = 8¾″ cut width for each tier

Determine the length of each tier

Now that you know how wide to cut each tier, let's figure out how long each tier piece needs to be. First, you need to figure out the circumference of each tier, but that's easy. Then you'll break the tiers down into cut sizes.

Each tier will be 1½ times fuller than the tier above it. So multiply the length of the yoke by 1.5 to figure out the circumference of the first tier. Round up to a whole number.

Each subsequent tier is 1½ times the length of the previous tier.

Example: For a yoke that measures 43":

43" × 1.5 = 64½". Round up to 65".

The first tier will be the cut width you calculated earlier × 65" long. The length of the second tier will be 65" × 1.5 = 97½". Round up to 98".

Repeat this to determine the length of each of the 5 tiers.

Figuring out how much fabric to buy

You'll be cutting lots of strips the width of the tiers, sewing them all into one strip, and then cutting them to the length you need for the tiers. I'll tell you how to figure out how much fabric you need to do this.

1. Add up all the tier lengths to get the total length needed.

2. Divide that total number by the width of fabric to determine how many strips you need to cut.

3. Add an extra 1¼" for each seam (1 less than the number of strips).

4. Multiply the number of strips by the cut width of the strips—don't forget the yoke! Divide that number by 36 to determine the yardage needed for your skirt. Buy a little extra just in case!

Example:

1. Tier 1: 65" + Tier 2: 98" + Tier 3: 147" + Tier 4: 221" + Tier 5: 332" = 863" total length needed for tiers.

2. 863" ÷ 52" width of fabric = 16.59 or 16 full strips and 31" of a 17th strip

3. 17 strips − 1 = 16 seams × 1¼" = 20". If your fabric is narrow, you may need to cut 1 more strip to account for the seams.

4. 17 strips × 8¾" = 148¾" + 5" for the yoke = 153¾"

153¾" ÷ 36 = 4.27, rounded up to 4½ yards needed

cut it out

Cut all the strips for the yoke and all 5 tiers using the cut sizes you determined in Take Your Measure (page 93).

Putting It Together!

All seams are ⅝" unless otherwise stated. Backstitch at the beginning and end of each seam. Press the seams open after sewing.

1. Sew the 5"-wide yoke right sides together at the short ends to make a loop. Finish the seams. Turn right side out. Set aside. **Figure A**

A

2. Sew all the tier strips, right sides together, into 1 long strip. Finish the seams. From this strip, measure and cut strips to the length of each of the 5 tiers.

3. Repeat Step 1 to sew the short ends of each tier strip together to make a loop, being careful not to twist your ever-getting-longer strip. **Figure B**

B

4. Run a gathering stitch (see Surefire Gathering, page 16) along the top edge of each tier. **Figure C**

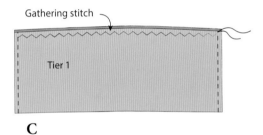

C

5. Fold the yoke in half, front to back, and mark with pins at the bottom edge. Fold in half in the opposite direction and mark in quarters. **Figure D**

6. Repeat Step 5 on the top edge of Tier 1.

7. Now it's time to attach the first tier to the yoke. With right sides together, match up the pins on the yoke with the pins on the tier and pin together in quarters. Pull up the gathering threads so the first tier fits the yoke, evenly distributing the tiny pleats. Pin all around and sew. Finish the seam allowance with pinking shears or a zigzag stitch. **Figure E**

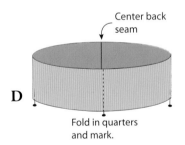

D

Fold in quarters and mark.

8. Repeat Steps 5–7 to mark, gather, pin, and stitch each additional tier to the skirt. Be mindful to keep the tiers right sides together while sewing. Also be careful not to twist the ever-growing tiers.

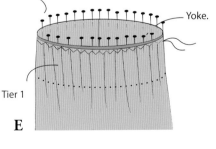

E

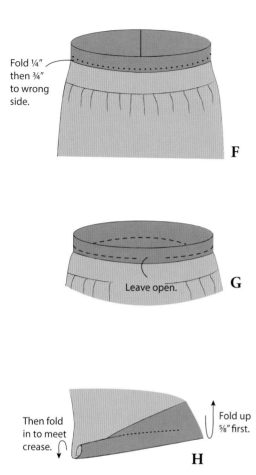

Fold ¼"
then ¾"
to wrong
side.

F

Leave open.

G

Then fold
in to meet
crease.

Fold up
⅝" first.

H

9. Make the casing in the yoke by folding the raw edge at the top over ¼" to the wrong side. Press. Fold and press over an additional ¾" to the wrong side. Stitch all around, close to the bottom fold, leaving an opening at the back. **Figures F & G**

10. Cut ½"-wide elastic 1" less than your waist measurement. Run the elastic through the casing with a safety pin or bodkin, making sure the elastic doesn't twist.

tip

Put a safety pin in the elastic and check the fit at this point, before sewing together the elastic.

11. Overlap the ends of the elastic about ½" and zigzag stitch across them several times. Push the elastic back into the casing and sew the opening closed. Put your skirt on and adjust the casing so that it is gathered evenly all around the elastic. Safety pin the elastic in place at the sides, and then stitch across the elastic to hold it in place and prevent it from twisting.

12. Hem the skirt by folding and pressing the bottom tier over ⅝" to the wrong side. Fold and press in the raw edge to the wrong side again to meet the crease. Stitch close to the upper fold. **Figure H**

Your skirt will be smashing!

TURNABOUT BLOUSE

Sizes from XS to XL
FINISHED LENGTH: **XS:** 24⅛″ **S:** 24¾″ **M:** 25⅜″ **L:** 26″ **XL:** 26⅝″

This delightful "big shirt" is as easy to make as it is to wear! I especially love the curved shirttail hem. It's called the Turnabout Blouse because it does just that—wear it either way because the front and the back are shaped exactly the same! If you're making view B with the contrast yoke, feel free to wear the yoke in the front or back! Why not sew three little buttons down the front of the pleat on view A?

SEW *clever!*

Because view B doesn't have a pleat, the neck is wider. I suggest wearing a cute camisole or tank top underneath for modesty and added color.

what you'll need

- **Turnabout Blouse pattern:** pullout page P1

- **View A (with pleat):** 1¾ yards of mid- or light-weight fabric, including rayon or voile

- **View B (with contrast yoke):** 1⅜ yards of mid- or lightweight fabric, including rayon or voile, for body and ½ yard of another for contrasting yoke

- **Single-fold bias tape:** 1¼ yards

- **Twill tape, ¼″ wide:** 1¼ yards

- **Pattern paper:** to trace original

Take Your Measure

Refer to the chart below to find your pattern size.

Trace your size of the blouse pattern onto pattern paper and cut it out, making sure to transfer all the markings.

Size:	XS (2/4)	S (6/8)	M (10/12)	L (14/16)	XL (18/20)
Bust:	35″	37″	40″	45″	48″

cut it out

- **Turnabout Blouse pattern, view A:**
  Cut 2 on the fold.

- **Turnabout Blouse pattern, view B**

  Main fabric: Cut 1 on the fold; then fold the pattern piece along the B line. Cut 1 lower body on the fold, cutting ⅝″ *above* the B line to add a seam allowance.

  Contrast fabric: With the pattern still folded on the B line, cut 1 yoke on the fold, cutting ⅝″ *below* the B line to add a seam allowance.

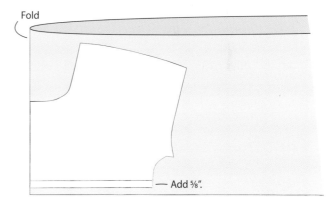

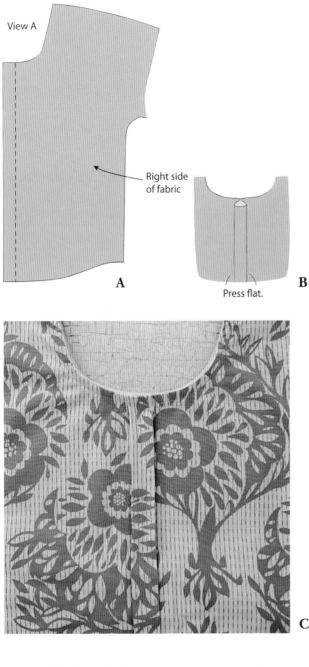

View A

Right side of fabric

A

B

Press flat.

Stitch yoke and body together.

C

D

Putting It Together!

All seams are ⅝" unless otherwise stated. Backstitch at the beginning and end of each seam. Press the seams open after sewing.

View A

1. Keeping the piece folded in half, wrong sides together, use tailor's chalk or a disappearing-ink marker (test on a scrap of your fabric first!) and mark every few inches along the pleat line for view A.

2. Pin in place and sew through both layers right on the line. **Figure A**

3. From the right side of the blouse, press the pleat flat, centered on the seam. **Figure B**

4. Repeat Steps 1–3 for the other blouse piece. **Figure C**

View B

Pin and sew the contrast yoke to the lower body along the B line, right sides together. Finish the seam allowances and press them up. Topstitch right next to the seamline on the yoke. **Figure D**

Both views

1. Pin and sew together the blouse pieces along the shoulders and the sides, right sides together. Finish the seam allowances. **Figure E**

2. With the blouse wrong side out, pin and sew twill tape around the neck, matching the edge of the tape with the raw edge of the neckline. Overlap the tape a little bit at the ends and trim it off. Stitch around the neckline right in the center of the tape. This reinforces the neck so it won't stretch out. **Figure F**

3. Turn the blouse right side out. Open out the bias tape and match up a raw edge with the raw edge of the neckline, right sides together. Pin and stitch the bias tape to the blouse, all around the neckline, on the fold line closest to the edge of the blouse. Start and finish at a shoulder and trim the bias tape off when you near the starting point, leaving enough to fold the end under with a little overlap. **Figure G**

4. Fold and press the bias tape over to the wrong side, letting the prefolded edge tuck back underneath the twill tape. From the wrong side of the blouse, topstitch around the neck close to the folded edge of the bias tape. Make sure your bobbin thread will look good on the blouse fabric before you stitch! **Figure H**

5. At each arm opening, carefully fold and press the raw edges in ½″ to the wrong side, and then fold the raw edge in again to meet the crease (so you'll have a ¼″-wide double fold). Ease the fabric so it's as smooth as possible. Sew all around, close to the fold. You may need to adjust your sewing machine to its free-arm position to sew all around the narrow opening. Check your manual for how to do this. If you don't have a free arm, sew slowly and carefully, making sure not to catch another part of the sleeve, or just stitch the sleeve hems by hand invisibly. **Figure I**

6. Fold and press the bottom of your blouse over ⅝″ to the wrong side. Tuck the raw edges in to the wrong side again to meet the fold. Ease in any fullness at the curves, press, pin, and sew all around the hem close to the upper fold.

Turnabout ... and wear this blouse to your next favorite activity!

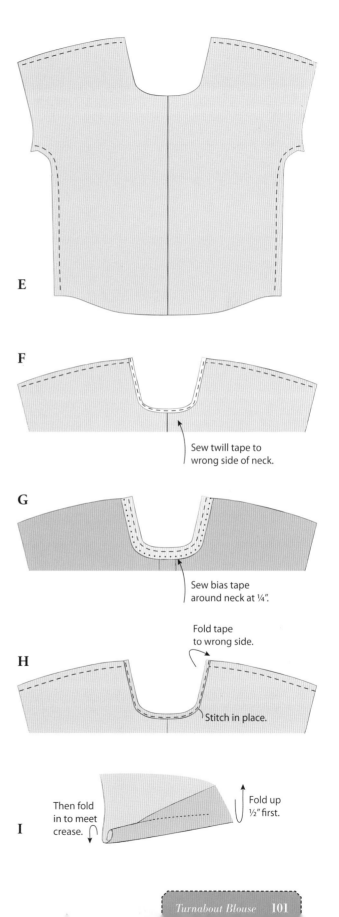

E

F

Sew twill tape to wrong side of neck.

G

Sew bias tape around neck at ¼″.

Fold tape to wrong side.

H

Stitch in place.

I   Then fold in to meet crease.   Fold up ½″ first.

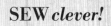

SEW *clever!*

Try lengthening the Turnabout Blouse to make it into a tunic! Figure out how much longer you'd like your tunic. Simply cut the pattern apart on the B line, and tape a piece of pattern cut to that length in between. Extend the lines for the side seams, connecting the yoke to the body.

A

B

SEW *clever!*

Make a Party Frock Belt out of contrasting or matching fabric to wear over your Turnabout Blouse. Why not?

CHAPTER 4: *home*

LEEWAY APRON

Fits most.

Whether it's strawberries and shortcake for break-fast or personal pan pizzas for supper, the Leeway Apron is sure to keep you absolutely clean while you have fun cooking.

what you'll need

- **Leeway Apron pattern piece:** pullout page P2

- **Midweight cotton or home decor fabric or large vintage tablecloth:** 1 yard or tablecloth at least 32″ × 50″ for apron body

- **Midweight cotton:** ¼ yard for pocket, straps, and ties

- **Double-fold bias tape:** (store-bought or self-made) 7 yards

This is the only project where you'll be making half of your own pattern piece.

Draw a rectangle 11¾″ wide × 21½″ high on a piece of freezer or tracing paper. Trace the Leeway Apron pattern (pullout page P2) for your apron top. Cut out the pieces and tape a narrow end of your own pattern piece to the bottom of the traced apron top pattern. It is ready to use!

cut it out

- **Leeway Apron pattern:** 1 on fold

- **For pocket:** 1 piece 12¾″ × 19½″

- **For waist tie:** 2 pieces 3½″ × 26″

- **For longer neck strap:** 1 piece 3″ × 26″

- **For shorter neck strap:** 1 piece 3″ × 12″

SEW *clever!*

Make your own bias tape. Cut enough strips of fabric, 1½″ wide, at a 45° angle across your fabric, to equal at least 80˝. Stitch the strips together at the short ends. Fold the raw edges in like you would for Loopie Loops (page 24) and Handles and Straps (page 25). Follow the directions to attach just like you would the store-bought double-fold bias tape.

Putting It Together!

All seams are ½″ unless otherwise stated. Backstitch at the beginning and end of each seam. Press after sewing each seam.

1. Make the neck straps by folding the 3″-wide fabric strips lengthwise, wrong sides together, so that the raw edges meet in the center. Press. Fold in half again so the raw edges are hidden and press again. Open up the strip, fold a short end over ¼″ to the wrong side, and press again. Refold along the middle. Stitch along the turned-under short end and the long open side. Repeat for the second strap. **Figures A & B**

2. Make the waist ties by folding the 3½″-wide strips in half lengthwise, right sides together. Stitch along a short end, pivot at the corner, and stitch down the length along the raw-edge side. Trim the corners and turn right side out. Press. **Figure C**

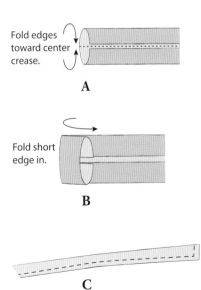

Fold edges toward center crease.

A

Fold short edge in.

B

C

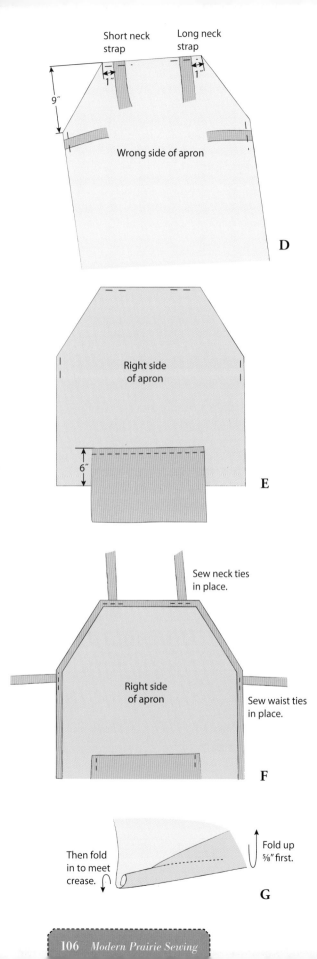

Short neck strap

Long neck strap

1"

1"

9"

Wrong side of apron

D

Right side of apron

6"

E

Sew neck ties in place.

Right side of apron

Sew waist ties in place.

F

Then fold in to meet crease.

Fold up ⅝" first.

G

3. With the wrong side of the apron up, and matching the raw edges, pin and sew the longer neck strap 1" in from the upper right corner as shown. Pin and sew the shorter neck strap 1" in from the upper left corner. Pin and stitch a waist tie at each side of the apron, 9" down from the top. You may want to stitch back and forth a few times in each place. **Figure D**

4. See Pockets (page 23) to make and attach the pocket 6" up from the bottom of the apron and centered from side to side. **Figure E**

5. Starting along a side at the bottom of the apron, encase the raw edge of the apron with the bias tape, pin in place if needed, and stitch through all the layers close to the inner edge of the bias tape. Continue up the side, across the top, and down the other side. The neck straps and waist ties will still be on the wrong side of the apron, facing down (or in).

6. After you sew down the bias tape, pull the neck straps up so that they face out (instead of down). Machine stitch through the bias tape across each neck strap. Repeat this step for the waist ties. **Figure F**

7. Fold and press the bottom of your apron over ⅝" to the wrong side. Fold and press the raw edge in to the wrong side again to meet the crease. Sew close to the upper fold to hem the apron. **Figure G**

With the apron finished, it's time to
make chocolate marshmallow bars.
Immediately!

PASS THE HAND TOWEL, PLEASE!

FINISHED SIZE: 14½″ × 23½″

When it's time to work in the kitchen, it's fun to see something that you've made—even when it's just a hand towel. These are so much fun to make! Be creative with your fabric combinations. Maybe you'll want a matching hand towel and oven towel set. Cute! And a nice gift.

what you'll need

- **Main cotton or linen fabric:** ½–¾ yard
- **Accent cotton fabric:** ⅛ yard
- **Matching thread**

cut it out

- **For towel:** 1 piece 16″ × 25″ of main fabric
- **For trim:** 2 pieces 1½″ × 16″ and 1 piece 1½″ × 25″ of accent fabric

Putting It Together!

All seams are ¼″ unless otherwise stated. Backstitch at the brginning and end of each seam. Press after sewing each seam.

1. Fold and press the long sides of the 3 trim pieces in to the center, wrong sides together. **Figure A**

2. Take 1 of the folded 16″-long strips and place it, raw edges facedown, on the right side of the 16″ × 25″ towel piece, 3½″ in from 1 end as shown. Pin and stitch in place on both sides of the strip. **Figure B**

3. Place the 25″-long strip, raw edges facedown, 2¾″ from 1 long side of the towel as shown. Pin and stitch in place on both sides of the strip. **Figure C**

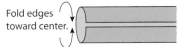

Fold edges toward center.

A

Towel, right side up

3½″

B

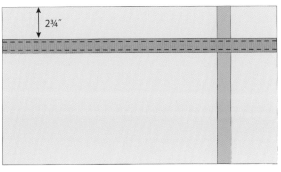

2¾″

C

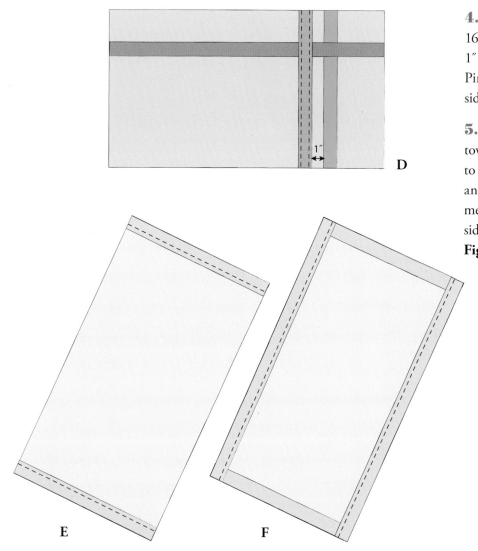

D

E

F

4. Place the remaining 16″-long strip parallel to and 1″ away from the first strip. Pin and stitch in place on both sides of the strip. **Figure D**

5. Hem all 4 sides of the towel at ¾″ (fold and press ¾″ to the wrong side, then fold and press the raw edge in to meet the crease). Do the short sides first, then the long sides. **Figures E & F**

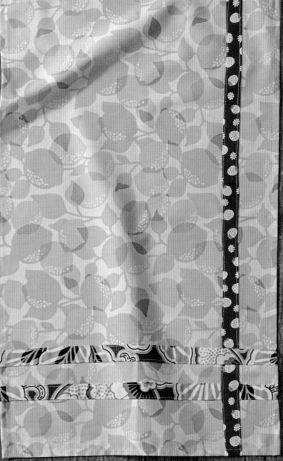

Towels too pretty to touch? No! Towels too cute not to use!

OVEN TOWEL

FINISHED SIZE: 6½″ × 10½″ (when buttoned)

People frequently flip a kitchen towel over the oven door handle for convenience. It's not so convenient when the towels end up on the floor. But this perfect little pal won't slip off as you run about the kitchen, going from one thing to the next!

SEW *clever!*

Why not replace the main fabric towel piece with a favorite store-bought kitchen towel cut down to fit?! If you've found the perfect color or pattern, go with it!

what you'll need

- **Oven Towel pattern piece:** pullout page P2
- **Cotton fabric:** scraps or ½ yard (if using just 1 fabric)
- **1 button:** ⅞″ in diameter

cut it out

- **Oven Towel pattern:** cut 2
- **For towel:** 1 piece 11″ × 15″
- **For trim:** 1 piece 1″ × 11″
- **For button loop:** 1 piece 1½″ × 3½″

Putting It Together!

All seams are ½″, unless otherwise stated. Backstitch at the beginning and end of each seam. Press after sewing each seam.

1. Make a button loop (see Loopie Loops, page 24).

2. Pin the button loop on the top of an upper towel piece, as marked on the pattern. Stitch in place. **Figure A**

3. Fold and press the bottom edge of both upper towel pieces over ⅜″ to the wrong side. **Figure B**

4. Pin the upper towel pieces right sides together, aligning the corners at the top and the folded edges at the bottom. Sew from the bottom fold up the side, pivoting at the top corner, and down to the other fold, leaving the bottom open.

5. Trim the corners, clip the curves, and turn right side out. **Figure C**

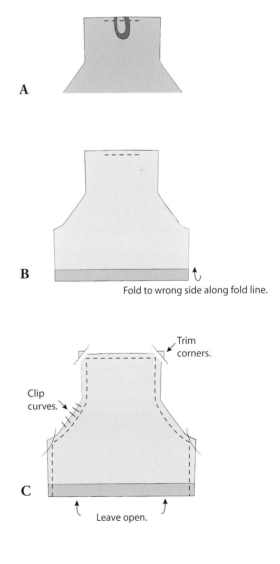

A

B

Fold to wrong side along fold line.

Trim corners.

Clip curves.

C

Leave open.

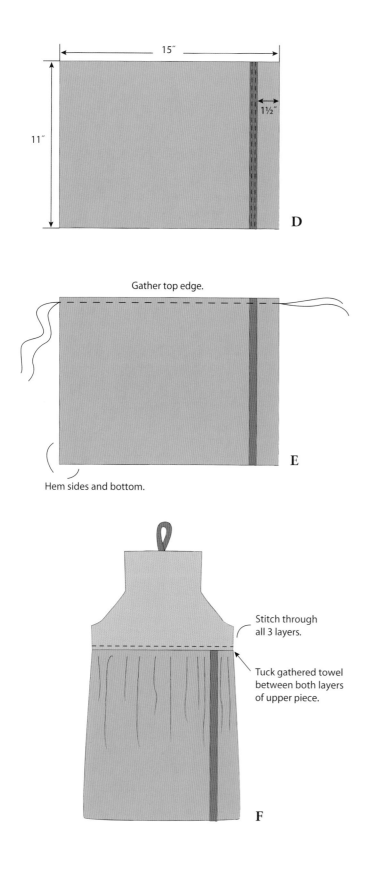

15″

1½″

11″

D

Gather top edge.

E

Hem sides and bottom.

Stitch through
all 3 layers.

Tuck gathered towel
between both layers
of upper piece.

F

6. Fold and press the long sides of the trim piece in to the center, wrong sides together.

7. Place the trim, raw edges down, on the 11″ × 15″ towel piece as shown. Topstitch both sides of the trim. **Figure D**

8. Hem the shorter sides of the towel with a narrow hem (see Narrow Hem, page 26). Then hem a long side. See Surefire Gathering (page 16) to run a gathering stitch on the other long side. **Figure E**

9. Gather the top of the towel to fit the opening at the bottom of the oven hand towel piece. Pin in place inside the open bottom of the assembled upper towel, so that the gathers are just hidden. Stitch through all 3 layers ⅛″ from the bottom of the upper towel. **Figure F**

10. Sew the button in the center of the upper towel piece, ⅝″ above the bottom seam. **Figure G**

G

Even if my cakes don't come out right, I know my cute hand towels never fall flat!

PIECES AND LETTERS PILLOWCASE

FINISHED SIZE: 21″ × 29¼″ (fits a standard pillow 20″ × 26″)

These pillowcases were so fun to make that I didn't want to stop! The Pieces and Letters Pillowcase is perfect for beginners and makes a fabulous gift. I love to use initials when I'm making these for my friends, but if you want to forgo the letters altogether, the fun patchwork still makes this unique!

what you'll need

- A mix of small and large fabric scraps, to total about 1 yard

cut it out

Before cutting your scraps, look at the pillowcase diagrams (page 119) and think about which fabrics you will use where. Label the pieces with their letters after cutting, for easier assembly.

- 1 rectangle 9¾" × 11" (A)

- 1 rectangle 2¾" × 11" (B)

- 1 rectangle 18½" × 11" (C)

- 1 rectangle 23" × 11" (D)

- 5 rectangles 7½" × 11" (E)

- 2 rectangles 9½" × 11" (F)

- 2 rectangles 7" × 11" (G)

- Strips 1½" × 8"–30" to make the letters

Putting It Together!

All seams are ¼". You don't need to backstitch, as most seams will cross each other. Press after each seam. I like to press my seams open.

1. To prepare the letter strips, press the raw edges of the 1½"-wide fabric strips so they meet in the center, wrong sides together.
Figure A

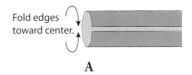

Fold edges toward center.

A

2. Let's make our letters! Decide which fabric rectangles you'd like to place the letters on, so you can make letters to fit. The letters should be at least ½" smaller than the fabric rectangle, if not more.

Most letters can be made with 1 or 2 strips.

For letters such as A, K, and F, you'll need 3 shorter strips. Place longer strips over shorter strips to cover the raw edges. Fold any short ends under ¼".

For letters with curves in them (such as J or B), ease the curves in. Just play around a little!

3. When you're happy with how your letters look, pin them in place on the fabric rectangles, both right sides up. Sew the letters in place by stitching all around the edges. **Figures B–E**

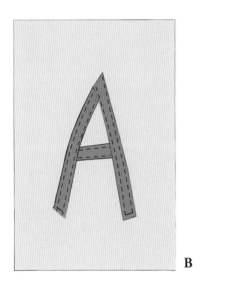

B

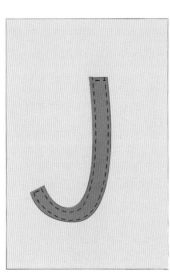

C

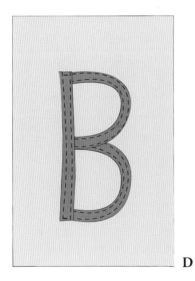

D

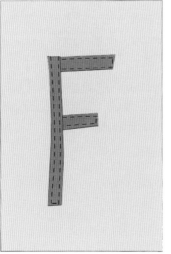

E

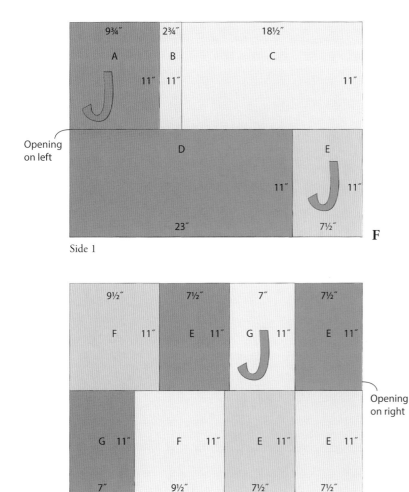

9¾" 2¾" 18½"

A B C

11" 11" 11"

Opening on left

D E

11" 11"

23" 7½"

F

Side 1

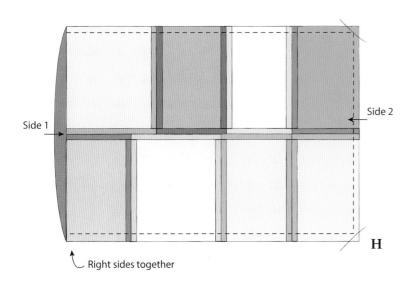

9½" 7½" 7" 7½"

F 11" E 11" G 11" E 11"

Opening on right

G 11" F 11" E 11" E 11"

7" 9½" 7½" 7½"

G

Side 2

Side 1

Side 2

H

Right sides together

Pillowcase layout

1. Now that your letters are in the right spots and looking terribly adorable, start sewing the pieces together, following the pillowcase layouts for each side. First sew the rectangles, right sides together, in each row—A to B to C, and so on. Then sew the rows together. **Figures F & G**

2. Sew pillowcase sides 1 and 2, right sides together, around both sides and a short end, pivoting at the corners and leaving the other end open. Backstitch at the beginning and end of this seam. Trim the corners. **Figure H**

3. Fold and press the open end of the pillowcase over to the wrong side ½" and then fold and press the raw edge in to the crease. Stitch close to the inner folded edge to hem your pillowcase. **Figure I**

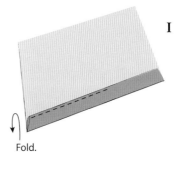

I

Fold.

Sweet dreams!

MEMORY QUILT

FINISHED SIZE: 75″ × 100″, a generous twin-bed size

Designed and pieced by Abigail A. Long, longarm quilted by Cheryl Comer

I can't count how many times we've found several of us all wrapped in the same quilt on a cold winter evening, watching a movie or just talking and laughing. We'd pull the same quilt out again in the summer for a fun Fourth of July picnic with friends. Whether it's a quilt made by my great-grandmother or one of my sisters, it's special because it was made with love. Quilts can hold the memories from 50 years ago or the memories from the previous night. This quilt will be no exception; it will hold memories, too. The simple design is very straightforward and easy to assemble. Snuggling under something you've made with love is extremely rewarding!

what you'll need

- **Memory Quilt pattern piece:** pullout page P2

- **Fabrics of various weights, including calico, voile, flannel, velveteen, and/or corduroy:** 3½ yards total for appliquéd shapes

- **Home decor–weight fabric:** 4½ to 6 yards for block backgrounds (If you can cut 4 squares across the width of your fabric, you'll need the smaller amount; if you can cut only 3 squares across it, you'll need the larger.)

- **Fabric at least 43″ wide:** 6 yards *or* a flat sheet, at least queen size, for backing

- **Cotton fabric:** 1 yard for binding

- **Batting:** 83″ × 108″

- **Perle cotton (if quilting by hand), yarn to tie, or machine-quilting thread**

tip

When deciding what fabrics to use for my appliquéd pieces, I chose different textures. I used smooth cotton and voile, as well as bumpy corduroy, furry velveteen, and fuzzy flannel. Feel free to mix textures to make a more interesting quilt.

cut it out

When you are planning your quilt and where to put what block, think of the textures and colors of the fabrics. You wouldn't want all your dark velveteen pieces at one end with your pale lightweight voile at the other. Make your quilt more interesting by having different colors and textures placed randomly throughout the quilt.

- **Memory Quilt pattern:** 24 circles from fabrics for appliqué

- **For appliqué:** 24 squares 9½″ × 9½″

- **For block backgrounds:** 48 squares 13″ × 13″

- **For binding:** 10 strips 3″ × width of fabric

Putting It Together!

All seams are ¼" unless otherwise stated.

Quilt top

1. Pin a circle or square to the center of each 13″ × 13″ background square, both right sides up.

2. Set your sewing machine to a wide zigzag stitch with a short stitch length. Zigzag around each individual circle and square, right over the raw edge, to appliqué it to the background square. Backstitch at the beginning and end. **Figures A & B**

3. Lay out the blocks on a large flat surface, starting in the top left corner with a square. Working left to right, make a row 6 blocks across, alternating squares and circles. Start the second row with a circle and the third row with a square again. Continue in this same pattern until you've used up all your blocks and have a 6-block × 8-block layout. You may have to move some around a bit until you've put them together in a way that appeals to your eye. **Figure C**

4. Sew each row of 6 blocks, right sides together. Press open each seam. After you've finished the first row, work the next row, and so on. After you've finished sewing each row, match the seams and sew the rows together lengthwise. Press the seams open. **Figures D & E**

A B

C Quilt layout

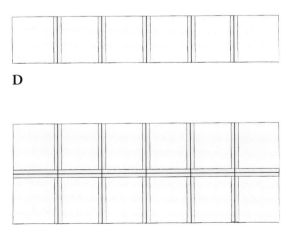

D

E

Quilt back

tip

If you've decided to take your quilt to a professional for quilting, before you make the backing and baste your quilt, ask your quilter how she would like you to bring it to her. Then skip to Binding It ... the quilters don't usually do that for you.

If using yardage for the backing

Cut the fabric in 2 equal pieces, each 3 yards long. Trim off the selvage edges. Sew the 2 pieces, right sides together, lengthwise. Press the seam open.

If using a sheet for the backing

Use your seam ripper to take out the stitching on the wide top hem of the queen-size sheet. Press out the folds.

For all quilt backs

Place the quilt backing, right side down, on the floor, and tape it down around the edges so it is taut. Place the batting on top of the backing piece, centered, and smooth out any wrinkles. Place the quilt top, right side up, on top of both, and smooth it out. Place safety pins through all 3 layers, a few inches apart, all over your quilt. Make sure the quilt backing, batting, and top are smooth and pucker-free after you've finished pinning them.

tip

Preparing your finished quilt top to become a finished quilt is exciting! Ask a quilting friend, or even chat with the sweet ladies at a fabric or quilt shop in your area, and ask them how they like to complete their quilts.

Quilting It

Entire books are written on quilting. I keep it simple, and this is just the bare bones of a quilting lesson.

By hand: If you've decided to quilt by hand, prepare your fingers for a shocker! For the rainbow design (below left), use a washable quilt marker and draw the rainbows accordingly. The best way to separate the rainbows is by drawing them in 4-block sets. You'll end up drawing 12 rainbows. (The quilt marker will wash out, but test it first.) Stitch small running stitches on the lines with a single strand of perle cotton or hand quilting thread.

By tying: Another simple way to finish your quilt is by using cotton crochet thread or wool yarn, taking a stitch through all the layers and knotting off in place. Repeat every few inches. Trim the thread/yarn ends about 1″ long.

By machine: If you're a beginner, try a straight stitch on your sewing machine. Go back and forth in little half-inch sections several inches apart on your quilt. There are all sorts of other ways to machine quilt as well that you can learn—long straight lines, wavy lines, or free-motion quilting, which requires a special sewing machine foot.

After your quilt is quilted, cut off the excess backing and batting, so that they're even with the quilt top.

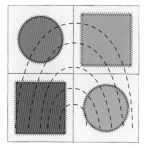

Hand-quilting pattern

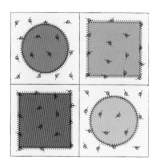

Tying your quilt

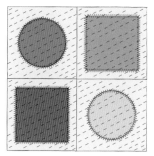

Machine quilting

Binding It

Now that your quilt is sewn together, let's bind all the edges.

1. Sew the short ends of the binding strips, right sides together, until you have more than enough to go all the way around your quilt. Press the seams open. Fold the whole strip in half lengthwise, wrong sides together, and press.

2. Starting not quite halfway along a side, pin the binding to the quilt top, aligning the raw edges. Leave a tail a few inches long before you start stitching. Stitch the binding on through all the layers with a ¼" seam allowance.

3. Stop stitching ¼" from the first corner and backstitch. Fold the binding up and then down as shown to make a mitered corner. Start stitching at the very edge of the quilt, backstitch, and continue until you've sewn the binding around all the edges of the quilt, stopping a few inches from where you started.
Figures A–C

4. Open up an end of the binding and fold the raw edge over a little bit to the wrong side. Overlap the binding, and cut the end off about 1" from the overlap. Tuck the other end of the binding inside the fold, and fold back in half again. Pin the binding down and sew the last section in place, backstitching at the beginning and end.

5. Turn the binding over to the back of the quilt. Use a slip stitch (page 18) to secure the binding to the back of the quilt. Use quilting thread for a strong finish. Pin or use binding clips to help you hold the binding in place while sewing.

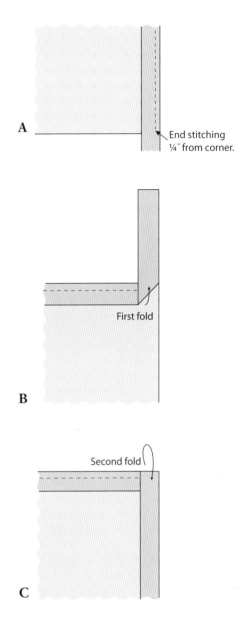

A — End stitching ¼" from corner.

B — First fold

C — Second fold

Make this little treasure and count the memories that follow.

ABOUT ABI

Abigail Long is a 20-something hands-on seamstress and crafter. She has been around sewing all her life and wants other young women to love it as much as she does! At an early age, Abi began experimenting with sewing techniques and making up projects, first for her dolls and then for herself.

Most days Abi can be found making a mess with fabric in her family's Missouri home studio, whipping up a yummy dessert, or goofing around outside with the family pets—a trio of collies named Blayde, Bo, and Brandy. Abi is a Christian, and her faith is an important part of who she is; it has contributed to her family values and how she views the resources of the world.

Read more by Abi at mariemadelinestudio.typepad.com, where she has written several sewing tutorials.

Resources

Fabric Manufacturers

These are great places to window-shop online, but they only sell to fabric shops. Note that most quilting fabrics are available for a limited time only, so you may not be able to find the exact fabrics I've used.

Michael Miller Fabrics
michaelmillerfabrics.com

FreeSpirit Fabric
freespiritfabric.com

LakeHouse Dry Goods
lakehousedrygoods.com

Fabric Shops

All of the gorgeous fabrics I've used are from these sweet places:

Marie-Madeline Studio
mariemadelinestudio.com
(My company—we also sell patterns!)

QuiltHome
quilthome.com

Suzie Q Quilts
suzieqquilts.com

Fabric.com
fabric.com

Other Supplies

Pellon interfacing
pellonprojects.com

Coats and Clark thread
coatsandclark.com

stashBOOKS

fabric arts for a handmade lifestyle

If you're craving beautiful authenticity in a time of mass-production...Stash Books is for you. Stash Books is a line of how-to books celebrating fabric arts for a handmade lifestyle. Backed by C&T Publishing's solid reputation for quality, Stash Books will inspire you with contemporary designs, clear and simple instructions, and engaging photography.

www.stashbooks.com